Off the
BEATEN TRACK

Off the
BEATEN TRACK

Irish Railway Walks

Kevin Cronin

Appletree Press

Published by
The Appletree Press Ltd
19-21 Alfred Street
Belfast BT2 8DL
1996

Author's Acknowledgements
There are three people in particular whom I would like to thank
for the tremendous help they gave me when researching and writing this book: Declan O'Driscoll, Dermot O'Sullivan and Patrick
Waterfield. I also thank those who accompanied me on the walks
and provided advice and useful assistance: Denis McHenry, James
Blair, Steve Lo, Adam Mannis, Michelle Minehan and Marie
McGowan. Special thanks to Philip Griffiths who helped with the
maps, and finally thanks to my editor, Douglas Marshall.

A catalogue record for this book is available
from the British Library.

ISBN 0-86281-563-0

Printed in Ireland

Contents

Burtonport

Ballycastle

Barnes Gap

Capecastle

Cloughan

Retreat

Glenties

Lough Mourne

Martinstown

Barnesmore

Tynan

Drumadonnell

Florencecourt

Maguiresbridge

Cornacloy

Fathom Forest

Newcastle

Westport

Greenore

Achill Sound

Walks

Location

Oughterard

Map

Aughrim

Clifden

Ennistymon

Tinahely

Kilkee

Miltown Malbay

Borris

Kilrush

Rathkeale

Glynn

Waterford

Lower Camp

Newcastle West

Glenagalt Summit

Donoughmore

Youghal

Dungarvan

Loo Bridge

Glenbeigh

Blarney

Killeagh

Morley's Bridge Waterfall

Cork City

Valentia Harbour

Passage West

Bandon

Map symbols

—— ► —— Route of Walk

———————— Public Road

〰 River

● Large Town

● Small town/Village

▬ Railway station building

◆ Miscellaneous Feature

▲ Mountain Peak (with height in metres)

⍦ Forest

⋈ Large bridge

Introduction

The Irish countryside is strewn with disused railway lines. Indeed, bearing in mind that nearly 3,200 kilometres of track has been shut down in this century, it is clear that there's a huge walking resource out there. Railway rambling is the enterprise of walking these abandoned trails.

This book is a walker's guide to some of the closed railways and in it you will find rambles on erstwhile busy provincial trunk lines, rural backwater branch lines, once frenetic suburban commuting routes and the scenic and remote western seaboard runs. Railway walks are distinctive, engendering a real sense of exploring lost and forgotten trails. The rambler encounters abandoned stations quietly returning to nature, long graceful curved viaducts now incongruously stranded on hillsides and impressive stone bridges hidden behind dense walls of foliage. Disused railway tracks will challenge and appeal to walkers of many backgrounds so get out there and get walking!

Irish Railway History

The first railway in Ireland was the Dublin to Kingstown Harbour (now known as Dun Laoghaire) line and was built in 1834. As in Britain, a railway mania quickly ensued and the network grew rapidly throughout the country during the nineteenth century. In areas that were predominantly agricultural, the railways in many cases provided people's first encounter with the industrial revolution. The pattern of railway development was very similar to that of the rest of the United Kingdom: numerous small independent companies operating modest railway lines were gradually absorbed by larger competitors so that by the turn of the century there were four or five dominant players. The years prior to World

War I saw the railways at their apogee in terms of prosperity and extent with total route mileage reaching its maximum of approximately 5,600 km. Every self-respecting town and large village was on the system and it would have been difficult to envisage the decimation that would occur over the next fifty years.

Notwithstanding their shared heritage, the railways in Ireland differed from their counterparts in Britain in two important aspects. The first was the gauge or distance between the rails. Parliament had decreed a gauge of 4ft 8½in for Britain and this width was also adopted on the Continent. However, in 1846, Ireland decided on a standard gauge of 5ft 3in, making the railways here unique in Europe. The second difference was the very considerable number of light railways that were built in Ireland, employing a narrow gauge of 3ft. The light railways made up 15 per cent of total national mileage and their widespread adoption was always regarded as a distinct characteristic of the Irish network. Their popularity is easily explained: the narrow gauge was more suitable and economical for railway construction in the sparsely populated rural parts of the country where the terrain was difficult.

The decline, and resultant contraction, of the rail system in Ireland was due to basic technological advances – the development of the internal combustion engine which lead to increasing, and ultimately strangling, road competition from buses, lorries and private cars. The unfavourable economic circumstances of the railways were exacerbated by unforeseeable economic and political factors. The population of the country, standing at over eight million at the outset of the railway era, had fallen to almost half this by the first quarter of the twentieth century. In addition, growing political dissatisfaction with the union with Britain culminated in the partition of the country: southern Ireland, eventually designated the Republic of Ireland, achieved independence in 1922 while six northern counties remained within the United Kingdom. Political upheavals at the time of secession impacted badly on all the railways and the advent of the border radically reshaped the economic geography of the country and further damaged railway profitability.

The worsening economic outlook of the rail system made closures inevitable. Outlying and the most unremunerative branch lines began to be shutdown in the 1930s, though the wholesale retrenchment of the system did not take place until the 1950s and 60s. The more severe cutbacks occurred in Northern Ireland where the Stormont Government, perhaps understandably, had a strong anti-rail policy. Another outcome of the deteriorating profitability of the railway companies was the eventual nationalisation of the networks in both the Republic of Ireland and Northern Ireland. Irish Rail operates the system in the former, while those in the latter are run by Northern Ireland Railways. Since the 1960s the position has generally stabilised and there is now about 2,400 km of operational track in the country. Indeed there is a modest renaissance in the fortunes of the Irish rail system due to substantial new investment in track infrastructure made possible by finance from Europe.

Abandoned Railway Lines
For a railway line to be declared abandoned the normal process is as follows. Passenger and freight services must have been stopped for a number of years before an abandonment order is obtained for the line. Rails, sleepers, signal posts and other equipment are removed for possible use elsewhere; bridges and viaducts may be taken down, either to make them safe or to remove the responsibility for their maintenance; rural station-houses and level-crossing gate-lodges are generally sold to the railway employees living in them at the time of closure; larger

stations in an urban environment may be sold to other businesses or converted into bus depots. The track bed itself is usually sold back to adjacent landowners for a nominal amount. As many lines in Ireland ran alongside the road, their reservations have frequently been incorporated into road-widening schemes. Some railway property is never purchased and is either demolished or left to decay. Obviously, once a line is broken up and the track bed sold on to several new owners, the natural linearity and associated right of way is lost and, apart from a few listed railway buildings, each new owner is entitled to do what they want with the land. Given that most of the abandoned lines in Ireland have been closed for over thirty years, track ownership is a very complex issue because of continuing development and alterations in land use.

There is no comprehensive law governing railway rambling but some points should be observed. Former railway lines are private property and, in theory, you should seek the owner's permission before you begin your walk. In practice, a more tolerant climate exists and, with responsible behaviour, you can ramble almost anywhere. You should be careful; avoid causing damage to any property that you are passing through and respect people's privacy. The legal position has recently changed in the Republic of Ireland with the passage of the Occupiers' Liability Bill. This is expected to improve access to the land by removing farmers' liability for trespassers. In my own experience, having completed a considerable amount of walking throughout the country, I have never found land-owners to be a problem. On a final point, it should be noted that it is a criminal offence to trespass on an operational railway line and should never be attempted.

In Britain, the attitude to abandoned railway lines has been more far-sighted than in Ireland. A comprehensive report drawn up in the late 1960s outlined people-friendly developments for dismantled railways and local authorities, using grants available from central government, converting disused track into footpaths, recreational trails and linear parks. These possibilities were sadly overlooked here which is a great pity as many of the old lines ran through the most scenic parts of the country, along the western seaboard. Some very short sections of track have been converted into public walkways, though in an ad hoc and uncoordinated manner. Recently, however, there has been growing awareness of, and enthusiasm for, the tourist resource presented by the abandoned network. There are a number of proposals to re-open lines as walking routes or to relay track on them for vintage steam runs.

Walk Planning

This book contains twenty-one routes, each of which corresponds to an original railway line, and comprises forty-one walks. On some routes only one walk is given, while others can have up to four separate walks. As far as is possible each stage or day of walking has been chosen so that it begins and ends at an appropriate point, both in terms of access to the track and availability of food and accommodation at the finishing point of each day's stage. A defining feature of railway rambling is its linearity; thus some form of transport will generally be necessary at the end of the walk to return to the starting point or to move further on. When walking alone, I generally use a bicycle in conjunction with a car. When walking in a group usually two cars are available which obviously facilitates matters. Some walks can be reached and returned from using public transport.

While the climate in Ireland means that you can walk at almost any time of the year, some periods are definitely more suitable for the special conditions pertaining to railway rambling. April, May, June and September are usually regarded as the best months for any outdoor walking. July and August can be uncomfortably warm and humid and, of course, the summer peak means that accommodation can be difficult to find. As railway rambling is across open country and not always on marked trails or firm paths, the most important climatic influence on walking is the rain. Wet conditions lead to very heavy going underfoot and railway reservations and cuttings are prone to becoming waterlogged and flooded. Starting your walk after a good dry spell is a huge advantage and should be borne in mind, whatever the time of year.

At the start of each stage description, the overall walk distance is given in kilometres and miles. If the distance is considerable and a sensible shorter alternative is available, it is also listed. Within the text, distances are given in metres though these are approximate and are only intended as a guide to the lengths involved. An estimated time for the duration of the walk is also supplied but this is obviously quite variable. The walking time that is given is reasonably conservative and allows for pauses to take refreshments and for admiring the sights, though it does not include prolonged or frequent stops. As a rough rule of thumb you could expect to cover an average of 3.2 km (2 miles) per hour though this can drop to 2 km or increase to 5 km, depending upon the condition of the line when walked.

Walking Tips
It must be remembered that old railway lines are not purpose walkways, but for the walks described in this book the track bed is in a reasonably good state for most of the route. Nonetheless, ramblers will meet obstacles on their journey and negotiating and surmounting these obstructions is one of the challenges of railway walking. Impediments can either be man-made or natural in origin: the former includes wire fencing and thick hedgerows laid across the track, new bungalows and farm outhouses built on the line, missing

bridges over rivers and streams, drainage channels cut into the track bed and torn-down embankments or infilled cuttings. Possibly the most serious man-made interruption is when landscaping makes the track unrecognisable. Natural obstacles include track beds overgrown with thick bramble and gorse, waterlogged cuttings and dense woods, which make forward progress very difficult. However, most obstacles are relatively minor and easily avoided by making a detour; where they are more serious the book makes specific suggestions.

Dealing with obstacles usually requires the application of a little common sense, but some general tips can be given. The most difficult task is to find the line; once you are on the track it is a straightforward matter to follow it. If the track ahead of you disappears, a sensible approach is to look behind you to gauge the direction that the line is taking and to carry on in this direction until the track bed reappears. An Ordnance Survey map showing the path of the old railway is extremely useful both for finding the track and for picking it up again after a prolonged interruption. In many cases, railway lines ran alongside roads and the latter can now be used to avoid obstructions on the track bed.

Waterproof boots are essential, but after that it is a matter of personal choice and the prevailing weather conditions as to what you should wear. Protection is advisable against thorns, nettles and gorse and I normally wear a denim jacket over a T-shirt with tracksuit bottoms. Loose-fitting clothes are not recommended as they inevitably catch in wire fencing and bramble hedges. It is also useful to carry a light raincoat in a rucksack together with a map, some food and of course your guidebook!

The walker should also bear in mind the following. Abandoned railway lines are not static and can change over a period of time, thus some information in this guide may become out-of-date. The walks in the book were carried out between April and June and the countryside can look considerably different at other times of the year. As it is not possible to provide an exhaustive written description of every walk, ramblers must be prepared to use their own initiative. Safety should not be a problem though care should be taken when passing over bridges and viaducts – assess their condition and be aware of the dangers of high winds. Where the book recommends that rivers be forded, they will be no more than 3 m wide and 30 cm deep. However, the walker must always use his or her judgement. Due to the stable geology of Ireland, tunnels should be safe, though falling masonry that has been loosened by water can occasionally present a danger. For long tunnels a torch is both comforting and essential to check the path ahead. Although bulls on farmland are not as common as they used to be, it's a sensible precaution to be on the lookout. Likewise, not all dogs are friendly.

Maps and Publications
Although each walk or stage is accompanied by a sketch map, it is advisable to carry the appropriate Ordnance Survey maps. The sketch maps I have included are intended only as outline guides; they are schematic and approximate with a scale included as an indication of distance. Ordnance Survey maps are especially important if, for whatever reason, you lose the trail and need to pick up the track again. A compass is not required for railway rambling though some walkers may find one useful.

At the time of writing the position regarding maps is somewhat confusing. There is an Ordnance Survey of Northern Ireland, based in Belfast, and another, separate body, the Ordnance Survey of Ireland, based in Dublin. Each publishes its own maps though they employ a common grid for the country. The Ordnance Survey of Northern Ireland produces a standard series of 1:50,000 scale maps, known as the

Discoverer series which covers all of Northern Ireland and contiguous parts of the Republic (including Donegal, Leitrim and north Louth) in 29 sheets. On these maps abandoned railway lines are indicated in considerable detail as a short dashed line and annotated "dismantled railway". The Ordnance Survey of Ireland produces maps for the whole country and their traditional standard series of half-inch scale (1:126,720) maps covers the island in 25 sheets. This series only shows operational lines and does not indicate the path of the old railway lines. Currently however, they are bringing out a new series using a 1:50,000 scale, known as the Discovery series which will replace the half-inch series but will not duplicate parts of the island that are already covered by the Northern Ireland Discoverer series. The new maps will depict the paths of all the old lines as a long dashed line with the annotation "dismantled railway". It will be a number of years before the remainder of the country is completely mapped with this new series, but almost all the walks listed in this book are available on an Ordnance Survey map.

For each stage of walking, an appropriate map is recommended. This can be either from the Northern Ireland or the Republic of Ireland series, depending upon the location of the walk. For Ordnance Survey of Ireland maps, either the half-inch series or the new Discovery series is suggested, depending on availability. Note that railway lines that were abandoned recently (i.e. within the past 15 years) or those lines closed but not yet abandoned, may be shown as operational lines in the half-inch series. Finally, well-stocked libraries should contain archive copies of Ordnance Survey publications that can also be used to trace railway routes.

There is a large volume of material detailing the history of the Irish railway network: books are devoted to individual railway lines, the narrow gauge system, pictorial guides and a national railway atlas. Personally, I have found

H.C. Casserley's well-written *Outline of Irish Railway History* to be an excellent source of information. While this guidebook is not a historical survey, I have given a brief note on the line each route follows to provide some context for the walker.

Accommodation and Transport
Almost every town, village and hamlet in Ireland can provide bed-and-breakfast accommodation during the summer season (Easter to the end of September), and even in wintertime there is seldom a problem. In addition there has been a large increase over the past 20 years in the number of hostels, though they are still not as comprehensive as bed-and-breakfast facilities. Booking ahead is not usually necessary except during the summer peak season, and the tourist boards in Northern Ireland and the Republic of Ireland can provide up-to-date information on accommodation through their local offices. Similarly, finding somewhere to eat at the end of the day is not usually difficult, though of course the number and availability of restaurants, cafes, pubs, fast food outlets and take-aways depends on the size of the town.

Public transport is not as extensive in Ireland as in other European countries; the existing rail service links the cities and most large towns, but buses are the most useful form of public transport when getting to or from railway walks. Bus Eireann in the Republic and Ulsterbus in Northern Ireland provide a reasonable service and their operation is augmented by many private bus companies. While Bus Eireann and Ulsterbus publish timetables regularly, it is more difficult to obtain timetables from the private companies and local enquiries are often the best approach. All the walks in this book are served by buses, though the infrequent service can make connections awkward.

Aughrim to Tinahely

The first public railway to be built in Ireland was a line from Dublin to Kingstown Harbour (now known as Dun Laoghaire) which was opened in 1834 by the Dublin and South Eastern Railway (D&SER). Over the next forty years the line was extended southwards down the east coast to Wexford. In 1865 a short branch line, leaving the main line at Woodenbridge station near Arklow, was opened. The line ran for 25 km, climbing up a river valley to Aughrim before turning south-westwards and continuing through Ballinglen, Tinahely and Shillelagh, where it terminated. In its heyday, at the turn of the century, the service provided a generous five trains each way daily, although contemporary reports complained that the worst engines were used on the branch. Decline quickly set in and, possibly exacerbated by war shortages, the route was closed in 1944.

Given its length, the branch should ideally provide two good consecutive days walking. However, from Woodenbridge to Aughrim the line traverses thick, deciduous forestry and the going is very tough in parts and strictly for the enthusiast! Similarly at its western end, though the line is intact from Tinahely to Shillelagh, it is very overgrown with bramble and thorn and actually impassable. Therefore I have decided upon a central stage, from Aughrim to Tinahely, as a one day ramble. It is a clear walk through a valley at the southern end of the Wicklow mountains. A good base is the coastal town of Arklow, which is still on the rail network, or any of the three villages on the branch line itself: Aughrim, Tinahely and Shillelagh. Nestling in the Wicklow foothills, they resemble the appearance of the Pennine villages in the north of England with their handsome granite stone buildings.

Maps: OS (ROI), Sheet 62 (Discovery series); OS (ROI), Sheet 19 (half-inch series)

Distance: 12 km.
Time: 4 hours.
Start: Aughrim village.
Finish: Tinahely station, 1 km east of the village.
Description: A distinctive walk through the wooded hills and attractive villages of south Wicklow.
Shorter alternative: Aughrim to Ballinglen (8 km).

Aughrim station stands on the other side of the Aughrim River from the village itself. The station house and platform are on the Tinahely Road (R747), hidden behind some large rhododendron bushes. The granite goods-shed with its over-hanging roof is further along the track and is now home to a Skoda garage. For the first kilometre the track runs beside the road to Tinahely through mixed woodland. I would advise walking this initial portion on the road and then joining the track when it becomes a clear embankment in a small forest plantation. The trail advances between the road and the Derry Water, an upper tributary of the Aughrim River, as a grass track coated with bluebells and buttercups. On the approach to Annacurragh you come across a willow copse, on an almost manicured grass embankment, and the track passes under a square stone bridge just to the south of the small village.

Leaving Annacurragh, the track bed runs through the wide open valley of the Derry Water for 5 km to Ballinglen station. It is overlooked by Croghan Mountain which lies at the southern limit of the Wicklow mountain range. The surrounding hills are covered with forest plantations and the area is the centre of an intensive forest products industry.

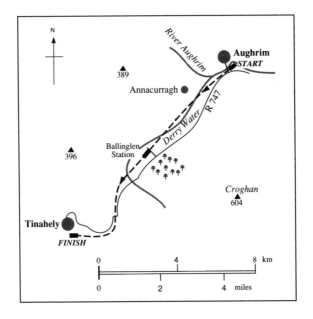

The rambler initially negotiates a narrow winding cattle trail between some tall hedges, but then the track opens out to a wide (nearly 20 m), grassy reservation. There is some gorse and pockets of nettles and thistles on the track, but plenty of room to avoid them. Indeed, given that the line was only single track, it seems somewhat profligate of the company to have demanded such a broad reservation. Two inlets of the Derry Water must be crossed with the aid of the remaining girderwork of the partially dismantled culvert bridges. Old railway lines are often a favourite haunt of rabbits, but this one is positively teeming with them and the Derry Water also has an abundance of wildlife. The track has been bulldozed into open fields for a long section along the river bank but traces of it, in the form of sleeper posts and farm-crossing gates, are still evident and act as useful signposts. Some other culvert bridges must be crossed and the track bed then returns to its original wide reservation bounded by white and pink hawthorn bushes and yellow gorse. The only awkward stretch of the journey occurs when approaching Ballinglen station; the walker is faced by a deep overgrown cutting but, by detouring through the adjacent fields, the station can be reached on the other side of a small road bridge. True to railway tradition Ballinglen station is over a kilometre from the hamlet of Ballinglen itself. The station consists of two dilapidated, though still inhabited, buildings and the platform has been subsumed under a number of absolutely enormous rhododendron bushes. It should have taken approximately 2.5 hours after leaving Aughrim to reach this stage.

The track continues through some fields but the Derry Water, which runs alongside the track, turns through a right angle, crosses under the track and turns away at this point. Unfortunately, the bridge has been removed and the river must be forded at a shallow point beside the remaining stone abutment. There is then an excellent stretch of track through a long poplar grove with crunchy ballast underfoot. The way becomes slightly overgrown when the poplar is replaced by willow and silver birch trees but then clears up to run as a wide and shallow cutting between clay walls. There are wild flowers on the track bed and the walker's progress is unchecked except for some low overhanging trees. As you draw near a road-bridge the trail becomes rough and boggy and walkers might prefer to take the adjoining road. Beyond the bridge the track is impassable: very overgrown with young spruce planted on it. Stay on the road for a kilometre and then rejoin the railway line by cutting through a field. The track soon arrives at Tinahely station, which consists of a stone goods-shed, a red-brick station house and a long platform.

They are all in a derelict condition though the goods-shed is currently being restored. There is a road bridge beyond the station from which you can see the Blackstairs Mountains to the south. Tinahely village, cosily ensconced in the hills, is 1 km away to the west, and Black Tom's pub in the attractive village square is a suitable location to rest your legs and replay the day in your mind.

Borris to Glynn

etween 1858 and 1873 a line was built from Baganels-
town (also known as Muine Bheag) in Carlow to
Macmine Junction near Wexford town. There were a
number of small, intermediate stations at Goresbridge, Borris,
Ballywilliam, Palace East and Chapel. At Macmine Junction
the railway made a connection with main Dublin-to-Wexford
line. The track straddled the operating spheres of the Great
Southern and Western Railway (GS&WR) and the Dublin and
South Eastern Railway (D&SER); the section of the line from
Baganelstown to Palace East was run by the GS&WR while the
remainder was under the control of the D&SER. In 1887 an
extension was built, leaving the line at Palace East, carrying
on to New Ross and continuing as far as Waterford city.
Service frequency was good in the early decades of this
century, with Bradshaw's timetable (for the GS&WR portion)
listing three trains to Borris daily and an additional train to
Palace East. As part of the rationalisation of the rail network
in the south-east, passenger services on the Baganelstown to
Macmine line were withdrawn in 1931 and the railway was
closed in 1963.

A one-day walk has been selected in south Carlow, from
the village of Borris to a point near the small hamlet of
Glynn. The track runs close to the broad and navigable River
Barrow, which forms the boundary between the countries of
Carlow and Kilkenny. It is one of the most scenic areas
in Leinster, with the Barrow valley sandwiched between
the Blackstairs mountains on the Carlow/Wexford border
and the large mass of Brandon hill in south Kilkenny.
Accommodation can be found in the villages of Borris and
Graiguenamanagh or at the town of New Ross to the south.

The impressive iron girder bridge that carried the New Ross extension over the River Barrow still stands 2 km north of the town; the middle portion of it has a swing section to allow for the passage of boats. A fine view of the bridge can be had from the Enniscorthy road (N79).

Maps: OS (ROI), Sheet 19 (half-inch series).

> **Distance:** 10km.
> **Time:** 4.5 hours.
> **Start:** Borris station.
> **Finish:** A road overbridge north of Glynn.
> **Description:** A walk in a broad, scenic valley, though the going is difficult in parts.

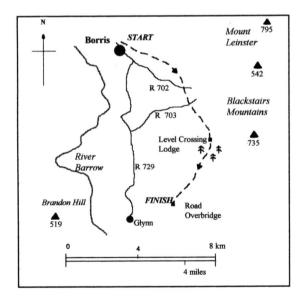

Borris is a small but attractive town in south Carlow with many quaint, old-fashioned pubs and shops. From the main street, walk down Pound Lane to Station Road. The stone station building is on your left, now serving as a private dwelling. Turning right and following along Station Road, an embankment at a dismantled road bridge appears and you can gain access to the track at this point. The embankment is in good condition, running parallel to the town's main street, though there is the minor inconvenience of two missing bridges over some foot paths. At the end of the embankment, walk across a sports field to reach a superb stone viaduct. It must be over 150 m long and provides tremendous views over the rolling, wooded countryside and on to the Blackstairs mountains whose tallest peak, Mount Leinster, is distinguishable by a TV mast on its summit.

Beyond the viaduct the track enters a long cutting that continues for almost 2 km. Hilly terrain always made railway construction difficult and this cutting, 10 m deep in parts, required extensive rock blasting. Unfortunately it has become overgrown in parts and it is necessary to walk through adjacent fields. You then pass two small road bridges and there is plentiful evidence of the original railway fence posting, with its characteristic thick iron wire. The cutting draws to an end and then the track becomes less discernible as it has in parts been landscaped back into fields. It runs in a continuous south-easterly direction and, luckily, both the telegraph poles built along the track and many farm level-crossing gates survive as a useful guide for the rambler.

A bridge remains where the railway track ran under the R702 and soon afterwards you come across the remains of a second bridge, where the track ran over the R703 road; this latter bridge has been substantially demolished. The trail curves to run in a more southerly direction, parallel to and less than 3 km from the Blackstairs' ridge line. The soil is quite sandy here and the entrances to a huge number of rabbit warrens are visible in the clay walls of the railway reservation. You pass an unremarkable level-crossing lodge at a small road, the only one on this walk, and the track enters a long shallow cutting. If this is wet you will be forced to walk along the sides of the cutting. The track approaches a spruce forest at which forward progress becomes easy as first a footpath and then a gravel trail have been laid on the track bed. While walking through the forest, I encountered an agitated farmer, out looking for calves that had got lost in the woods!

Leaving the forest, the track passes under a large overbridge which has been partially disfigured by the removal of some of its fine cut stone. The trail then follows a long and generally clear embankment which again permits good views over the countryside. The southern end of the Blackstairs mountains are on the eastern skyline while Brandon Hill in Kilkenny is to the west. A number of railway mileposts with distances enscribed on them can be seen at the side of the track and you then come upon another road overbridge. I finished the walk at the point due to the onset of evening though it may be more convenient for some walkers to continue the further 3 km to where the railway crosses the R729 road just south of Glynn.

Waterford City to Dungarvan

In 1878 the Waterford, Dungarvan and Lismore Railway Company (WD&LR) opened a line running from Waterford City, through Dungarvan and Cappoquin, to Lismore. The railway was part of the main line between Waterford and Cork and eventually became the direct route by which ferry passengers arriving at Rosslare travelled to Cork. In the early part of this century there were five trains a day, one being the boat express, but in 1967 it was decided to close the line and re-route Waterford to Cork trains via Limerick Junction. It was one of the last major lines to be closed, heralding the end of the great rationalisation of Irish railways. A section of the line, from Waterford to Ballynacourty, was re-opened in 1970 as a freight line serving a magnesite plant and a short, new spur was built which ran from the original track down to the plant on the sea-front. However, in 1981, even this freight line was closed.

The walk commences in Waterford City, which dates from Viking times and is situated on the south coast. It has good transport links with the rest of the country and copious accommodation, drinking and dining facilities. All of the walk is in County Waterford, and runs westwards from the city to the pleasing seaside town of Dungarvan. This line is unusual in that, although it has long been closed, it still awaits an abandonment order. It is owned by Irish Rail and the tracks, sleepers and ballast have not been removed yet. Thus there exists a marvellous opportunity to convert it into a purpose-built walkway as has been done with some of the old railway lines in Britain. Apart from certain sections that are infested with gorse, it is likely to prove one of the easiest lines to walk as it retains its linearity intact. The total walk is 46 km long and it can be completed in three days. The first stage leaves the city, follows the broad River Suir and then strikes off across country to Carroll's Cross Roads. The second stage is through the hilly terrain of central Waterford, passing through the southerly slopes of the Comeragh Mountains and finishing near the hamlet of Lemybrien. The final stage leaves the mountains and follows the west Waterford coastline into Dungarvan. Experienced walkers may prefer to finish the walk in two days, breaking at the small town of Kilmacthomas which is roughly half-way along the journey. *Maps: OS (ROI), Sheet 75 (Discovery series); OS (ROI), Sheets 22 and 23 (half-inch series).*

STAGE 1: Waterford City to Carroll's Cross Roads

Distance: 17.5 km.

Time: 4.5 hours.

Start: At the south side of the disused rail bridge over the River Suir.

Finish: Carroll's Cross Roads on the Waterford to Cork road (N25).

Description: An uninterrupted walk on the old track line along the River Suir.

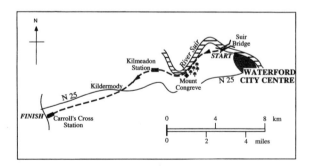

Bridge along the River Suir, County Waterford

Starting at the road-bridge over the River Suir, take the road westwards, along the south bank of the river, for just over 1.5 km until you meet the railway at a road underbridge. You should join the track at this point by clambering up the side of the bridge. It is worth walking the short distance back along the track to the large rail bridge for the view of Waterford, though the bridge itself is closed and you should not attempt to cross it. The walk proper now commences: the railway runs through a long cutting, crosses over a hill and then rejoins the river bank for 6.5 km. This stretch is popular with city ramblers and also with pupils playing truant from school! On the day I walked, a thick early morning mist hung over the river and the atmosphere was heightened by the ghostly voice of an unseen public address system echoing from a riverside depot. Gorse and brambles flourish on the side of the track but the path itself is clear, the only impediment being the well-known difficulty of developing a good walking rhythm on rail sleepers. Away from the city, the track is awash with birds and, to a non-ornithologist like me, their twittering and chattering sounds like furious Morse code. The track crosses a number of large iron bridges over tributaries of the Suir and numerous smaller stone culverts. The River Suir itself is over 300 m wide at this point and fast-flowing, and its muddy banks are covered in enormous reeds. The river also forms a county and provincial boundary; the northern banks are in County Kilkenny in Leinster, while County Waterford is in Munster.

As the Mount Congreve Estate is reached, the track runs alongside a very large garden centre. In parts the path is quite narrow, either due to river erosion or the nearby garden centre encroaching on the track. A rather comical episode took place here when I inadvertently disturbed a workman who had sneaked away to what he obviously thought was a hidden spot for a surreptitious cigarette. When he regained his composure he was quite informative about the line and the neighbouring estate.

Beyond the garden centre, the river and track part company as the railway curves away through some meadows. Many large, mature, deciduous trees have been planted here and in one deep, rocky cutting one tree had fallen over and blocked the line. Telegraph poles, level-crossing gates, stiles, square concrete fence posts with thick rusted wire – the usual paraphernalia of an old railway – are all present in the side hedges. The railway passes over a road and then under two road-bridges. The second of these is at Kilmeadon station, one of a number of very small stations on the line and the first stop after Waterford. The main Cork road is only 1 km away and there is a shop there and a pub which serves food. When I spoke to the few fellow walkers I met on the line, I learned that Kilmeadon is regarded as the western limit for city ramblers and, certainly, their numbers decline sharply after that station.

After leaving Kilmeadon, flowering yellow gorse appears alongside the track and remains a constant, and at times a most unwelcome, companion to Dungarvan. A long, straight section in a cutting leads the walker under another road-bridge and then a tall embankment carries the line over a steep river valley. The railway aligns itself along the north side of the main road (N25). From central Waterford on the terrain is quite hilly and severe grades, curves and cambers (by railway standards) were needed to thread the line to Dungarvan. The land here is more agricultural than the earlier river section and some cattle were already out in the fields at the beginning of April.

The railway crosses the main road at Kildermody, where a redundant gate-lodge remains on guard. The lodges on the line are easily recognised by their tall and narrow shape, though many of them have been renovated and extended by their owners. Continue along the line, past a garish advertising billboard, for another 3.5 km until you reach Carroll's Cross station. The track remains close to the main road, though now on its south side. It runs along hill ledges and embankments, heavily curved, cambered and, in parts, colonised by furze. A small road is crossed at Ross and the next level-crossing gate-lodge is in fact Carroll's Cross station, though, as it is even smaller than Kilmeadon, it should have been more accurately described as a halt. Carroll's Cross Road, on the main road, is 200 m away on the right and has a large pub which serves meals and snacks. A bus for Waterford and Dungarvan stops outside the pub twice a day.

STAGE 2: Carroll's Cross to Lemybrien

Distance: 14.5 km.
Time: 4.5 hours.
Start: Carroll's Cross station.
Finish: Lemybrien hamlet on the Waterford to Dungarvan
road.
Description: An uninterrupted walk along the southern
flanks of the Comeragh and Monavullagh Mountains.

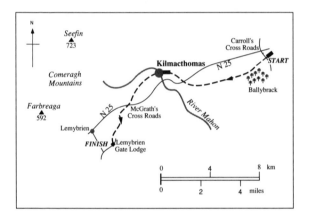

Immediately after Carroll's Cross station the track runs
through a large quarry and brick manufacture plant and the
railway tracks are submerged under layers of caked dust.
There is a level-crossing lodge situated just beyond the
quarry, on a small lane which runs down from Carroll's Cross
Roads, and if you take this slight detour, you can skirt around
the plant. The line then curves away from the main road and
passes a series of coniferous woods at Ballybrack. The track
leads up an incline until it reaches the level-crossing lodge at
Scrahan and then through a cutting which peters out in

green meadows. There is a very tall embankment here, 10 m high, which offers excellent views of the Comeragh Mountains. The hilly country continues and the track descends through a cutting with an old stone warehouse on your left. The main road is crossed again, this time by a bridge over the road, and the track curves as it descends into Kilmacthomas. On a good day, this is a very scenic section of the walk, as the track heads straight for the Comeragh Mountains. I met a senior citizen who uses the railway daily to walk from the village to his home, claiming that it is safer than the main road. He remembered as a young lad going with his mother to Cork on the steam trains and expressed the ubiquitous regret about the closure of the line. A schoolboy passed me by, returning home from the local school, and it struck me that the line continues to serve the local community, although not in the way intended by the railway builders.

The large station of Kilmacthomas, 6.5 km from Carroll's Cross station, is situated at the eastern end of the main street. There is a derelict station building, a goods-shed, a signal-box with the signal and points levers still intact, two platforms with a passing loop and a siding. Two pensioners were having a nostalgic afternoon strolling about the site; one of them remembered being a passenger on the line as far back as 1919. The village of Kilmacthomas itself, though the only centre of population between Waterford and Dungarvan, is something of a sleepy backwater and the shops retain the style of a previous era. The River Mahon flows through the village and there is an old woollen mill, which I admired before taking a well-earned break in a coffee shop. Kilmacthomas has several bed-and-breakfast establishments and good transport links to both Waterford and Dungarvan.

When leaving the station, the walker traverses a bridge over the road and then a long viaduct over the River Mahon. There is unusual reddish coloured stone in the track ballast as

The viaduct at Kilmacthomas, County Waterford

opposed to the more standard limestone or shale. The railway had a very steep ascent up and around a hill, through rock blasted cuttings, as it left the Mahon basin: a full head of steam must have been the order of the day for westbound trains. Primroses littered the track and sycamore and birch saplings showed the first sign of budding. The main road is crossed again, for the last time, at McGrath's Cross Roads. The rabbits, birds and yellow gorse were still ever present and sheep plentiful in the adjacent fields and on the track. Some farmers, anticipating the ultimate abandonment of the line, have already strung fencing across it. The path carries on over stone cattle-crossing bridges and a long embankment which provides an excellent view of Mahon Falls in the

Comeragh Mountains. At the next level-crossing gate-house, I spoke with the woman who lives there. Her forebears had all worked on the railway and both her sons, continuing the tradition, are employed by Irish Rail.

About a kilometre further on is another level-crossing over a small road. The actual crossing gates are still here though, of course, no longer used. The mountain range to the north is the Monavullagh Mountains, a westward extension of the Comeraghs. This is the closest point to Lemybrien, 1.5 km due west as the crow flies but twice that distance by foot! Turn right, continue down the road and bear right again at the Y-junction. Lemybrien hamlet, on the main Waterford road, can be summed up as having one shop, one pub, one bed-and-breakfast and a bus-stop. I took the country bus back to Waterford, a slow service due to numerous halts. It was amusing to note that anybody boarding the bus was immediately familiar with the other passengers and a constant jocular banter ensued, a personable contrast to more anonymous city life.

STAGE 3: Lemybrien to Dungarvan

Distance: 14.5 km.
Time: 4.5 hours.
Start: Level-crossing lodge, 1.5 km east of Lemybrien.
Finish: Dungarvan station (near the town centre).
Description: Railway track to the sea, though some sections after that are on the road.

After walking down a shallow cutting, a long, stone bridge carries the walker over a river valley. The chairs (cast iron objects connecting the rails to the sleepers) have the letters GS&WR and the date 1924 stamped on them, reminders of

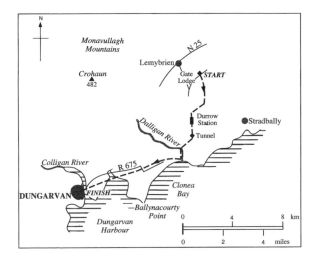

the Great Southern and Western Railway who took over the line from the Waterford, Dungarvan and Lismore Railway Company in the last years of the nineteenth century. The track runs over a small road at a level-crossing. Shortly after this you come to the last station before Dungarvan – Durrow & Stradbally. It is surprisingly large, consisting of two platforms, a station-house and   signal-box. The latter two buildings are still standing, but derelict, and the site is now adjacent to a fertiliser depot. It is a good example of the rural station "in the middle of nowhere", being over 3 km from the well-kept seaside village of Stradbally which it was meant to serve. This is not unusual – in the last century railway companies appear to have been unscrupulously adept at naming stations after centres of population that could be considerable distances from the train halts!

Leaving the station behind, numerous farm gates and stiles can be seen on either side of the track as the railway

heads south to the sea. The Comeragh Mountains still dominate the skyline behind you, an impressive backdrop to the
walk. The railway ascends an incline and then runs into a
deep rock cutting as it approaches Durrow tunnel. Long
tunnels were a rarity on Irish railways, largely because of their
cost. Durrow tunnel is straight and about 300 metres long.
As with most railway tunnels, the interior walls are lined
with brick and the recessed alcoves in the walls for railway
workmen are clearly visible. Tunnels in Ireland are usually
safe, the only danger being from loose masonry, though it is
advisable to carry a torch with you.

Coming out of the tunnel, the track proceeds through a
cutting and along an embankment which leads to the
Dalligan viaduct; there are magnificent views of Helvick
Head, on the other side of Dungarvan Bay. The railway
continues along a mountain ledge, following the Dalligan
river to the sea. The track then turns sharply westwards in a
grassy cutting, passing a shabby and derelict gate-lodge. For a
while it runs alongside Clonea bay so closely that you can
smell the seaweed. The beach lies before you, curving around
to Ballynacourty point, the site of the old magnesite factory.
The track then turns inland, closely paralleling the coast
road (R675) away from the sea. Some of the cuttings are now
so overgrown with gorse that the walker is forced to use the
road for a few sections.

The track passes under a road overbridge and curves
sharply southwards. From here on the rails are those which
belonged to the spur line built to serve the magnesite plant –
the original Dungarvan line continued on beside the road.
The line is now little more than a farm track: the rails,
sleepers and ballast have long gone and it is so overgrown in
parts that it is best to use the road for the next mile. While
walking towards Dungarvan another distinctive, tall and
narrow gate-crossing lodge can be seen on the left. A bizarre

road sign declaring this to be the "Gold Coast Amenity Area" and a clump of miscellaneous conifers, larches, pines and spruces are met just before the cross roads at Dungarvan harbour. The town centre is still almost 3 km away but the foresight of Dungarvan council has meant that the road is not required, as they have converted the track bed into a municipal walkway for this final stretch. A causeway and bridge leading the old line across the harbour can be reached by taking the road to the left at the cross-roads. From the bridge, the view to the right reveals the wooded Monavullagh foothills sweeping down to the coast while on the left are the Drum Hills on Helvick Head peninsula.

Beyond the causeway, the track proceeds as a tarmac path through the Dungarvan suburb of Abbeyside, then through a grassy cutting and under a road-bridge. In parts, it is heavily littered, betraying its urban environment, and is used as a path into town by the local inhabitants. The trail comes right into the river estuary at Dungarvan harbour where various fishing and sailing boats nestle on the water. After crossing the road at a row of shops, the track runs through a small park and over the Colligan River using the original rail bridge just upstream from the road-bridge. The station at Dungarvan, originally located just beyond the large Waterford Co-op plant, has unfortunately been completely obliterated by developers. It is a shame that such an interesting walk doesn't have a more appropriate climax.

Dungarvan is a worthwhile spot in which to spend the night. Developed as an urban centre by the Normans, its castle dates from 1185. Although not large, it has a wide selection of good pubs in its streets and along its quays. The town also has a sizeable collection of fish restaurants which nowadays seems to be mandatory for any Irish seaside resort. There are excellent bus connections back to Waterford or on to Cork.

Killeagh to Youghal

T he railway line from Cork City to the town of Youghal, 42 km to the east, was completed in 1860. There were also stations at Carrigtwohill, Midleton, Mogeely and Killeagh serving the east Cork region and initially there were plans to extend the railway all the way to Waterford, but this hope was never realised and Youghal became the terminus of the line. The important harbour of Cobh was connected to the railway via a branch line, located between Cork and Carrigtwohill, built in 1862. The Youghal line was initially operated by the independent Cork and Youghal Railway Company (C&YR) but was soon purchased by the much larger Great Southern and Western Railway (GS&WR). The line was integrated into their network and eventually the service to Youghal left Cork from Glanmire Road terminus, now known as Kent station. A preserved GS&WR locomotive, dating from 1848, is still exhibited in the concourse of Kent station. Passenger services to Youghal ceased in 1963, though goods were carried for some years after, but the line to Cobh is still operational for both passengers and freight. Despite the fact that some sections of track at the eastern end of the line have already been lifted, the Youghal line still awaits an official abandonment order from Irish Rail. There has also been some talk in recent years of restoring a commuter service to Midleton.

While part of the line has remained clear, other sections are very heavily overgrown and impenetrable, and so I have selected a single, short walk suitable for a day's ramble. It is from a point east of the small town of Killeagh to the station building at Youghal. Killeagh is well served by buses, lying as it does on the main road from Cork to Youghal (N25). The town of Youghal is similar to Bandon; both date from the Munster plantation era, a heritage which is plainly evident in their respective municipal architectures.

Map: OS (ROI), Sheet 25 (half-inch series).

Distance: 7.5 km.
Time: 2.5 hours.
Start: 3 km east of the town of Killeagh.
Finish: Youghal station.
Description: A short walk in the flat country of east Cork, ending at the seaside town of Youghal.

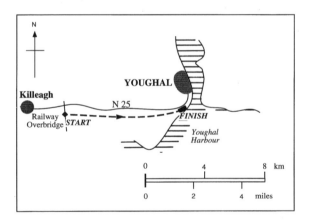

The station at Killeagh is surprisingly large and, although empty, remains in a quite good condition. However, beyond the station the track has reverted to an almost jungle-like condition and is not navigable, thus a slight detour is required to pick up the track at a suitable point. Head towards Youghal and when you reach the junction about 3 km outside Killeagh, take the road on the right. A short distance down this road there is a bridge over the railway and you can join the track at this point. Rails and sleepers are still present on the track, although most of the sleepers are decayed and rotten. The track lies to the south of the main road and a long ridge of low hills. It runs level between thick clay walls which have dense bramble and hawthorn hedges on top, before making its way through the rich, fertile countryside of east Cork. When I walked the line, there was an intense hum of bees and other insects and I even managed to photograph a baby fox on the track. The trail carries on under a foot-bridge, mostly clear of any obstructions except for the occasional gorse bush. Beyond the bridge the rails and sleepers have been removed but the walk continues on crisp ballast.

Presently views open up of the surrounding countryside as the side hedgerows disappear and stretches of the track lead on to raised embankments. Two bridges are passed, under and over respectively, and the road to Ballymacoda is crossed; the discarded crossing gates can be seen hidden in the grass. The approach to Youghal is almost reminiscent of the prairie country of the Russian steppes or the midwestern United States; the track runs perfectly straight and level on a low embankment through a swamp where the tall marsh grass stretches out in all directions. The tower on Capel Island in Youghal Bay can be seen to the south. At the outskirts of the town, you encounter caravan parks and the rails and sleepers reappear on the track bed as you travel under the last road bridge. The trail curves around a pitch and putt course and glides into Youghal station behind some seaside terraced housing. There is a large sidings yard and the station house, a long, red-brick building in the Romanesque-style which, although boarded up, still stands on its island platform. The station is right beside the large beach and fun fair at Youghal which must have made it very popular with day excursionists from Cork. The town itself is further around the headland on the Blackwater estuary. It was once an important port but later settled for being a coastal resort; the rows of large terraced houses with big bay windows overlooking the sea certainly retain the atmosphere of an Edwardian seaside getaway.

Cork City to Passage West

The railway line between Cork and Passage West opened in 1850 and was the first railway in Cork city. The main line from Dublin to Cork had been completed a year earlier, in 1849, but its terminus was to the north of the city limits. The Passage line was operated by the Cork Blackrock and Passage Railway (CB&PR) and ran from its headquarters on Albert Street, through Blackrock and Rochestown and on to Passage. The line was initially built to standard gauge but when it was extended from Passage to Crosshaven at the turn of the century, the railway was converted to narrow gauge. Between Cork and Blackrock the line was double track – the only occurrence of double track on a narrow gauge system anywhere in the British Isles. There were two important engineering constructions on the line: a bridge over the Douglas river estuary between Blackrock and Rochestown and a long tunnel after Passage. Unlike most narrow gauge railways in Ireland, which were in lightly populated rural areas, the urban setting of this line made it unusually profitable in its heyday. However, it proved very susceptible to competition from road transport, especially buses, and successive annual losses meant that the whole line was closed down in 1932.

The line between Cork and Crosshaven was 26 km. However, only the initial section, from Cork to Passage, is suitable for walking; the remainder of the line, running down the western side of Cork Harbour, is either overgrown or has been built on. The walk is unique in two respects; it is one of the very few disused lines in Ireland that runs in an urban environment and, over most of its course, it has been converted into a recreational trail. Unfortunately this conversion must have taken place in an ad hoc manner as there is no publicity or information to either advertise the walk or to place it in its historical context.

Maps: OS (ROI), Sheet 25 (half-inch series); also the Cork city street map.

Distance: 10.5 km.
Time: 2.5 hours.
Start: Albert Street, near City Hall.
Finish: At the centre of Passage West.
Description: A purpose-built walkway in an urban
    environment.

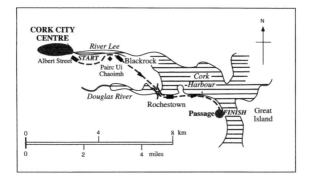

The terminus of the railway, a large, dog-leg shaped building that is now used by a builders' merchant, is located at the corner of Albert Street and Albert Road. This station is in close proximity to the former Bandon line station on Albert Quay, though the lines were entirely separate. After leaving the station the track runs down Albert Road and across the roundabout to Monahan's Road. About 100 m down the road the track bed appears, a wide grassy margin with a footpath.

The line runs through an industrial part of the city passing factories, warehouses and fuel depots, skirting the agricultural showgrounds and running right under the north stand of the Gaelic sports stadium, Pairc Ui Chaoimh. It continues for a short distance between the River Lee estuary and a parkland lake before the walkway proper commences, 2 km from Albert Street. The track runs on a wooded embankment, curving away from the River Lee through a residential area. Two road overbridges are soon met in quick succession and after the second bridge you come upon Blackrock station. The brick and stone station building is still present, but derelict, though the two platforms are in good condition.

The track then leads through a long cutting which is quite deep in parts and must have required considerable rock-blasting in its formation. There are some fine oak trees along the path. Indeed, the line seems to be a nature sanctuary in the midst of a man-made environment. For ramblers more accustomed to walking cross-country on disused rural lines, it is strange to find a track with so much "civilisation" in evidence. Two more road bridges are passed under and then the track crosses another road on the level. On the approach to the Douglas River the track gradually descends and the cutting peters out. The line crosses the southern city by-pass road and continues past a towering television transmitter. The Douglas River estuary is crossed by means of a metal girder bridge which was blown up by republican forces during the Civil War in an attempt to prevent Government troops, who had landed at Passage, entering the city. The line then enters the extended city suburbs of Rochestown, 6 km from the start of the walk. The station there is across the road from the Rochestown Inn, a large public house which serves as a local landmark. I broke the journey there and couldn't help but notice the dreadful doggerel, supposedly a tribute to the famous Cork hurler,

Christy Ring, displayed behind the bar! The station house now masquerades as an anonymous suburban dwelling, but its original purpose is betrayed by its red brick chimneys.

Unfortunately, for the next 250 m the track disappears and the footpath on the main road must be taken. The walkway materialises again at the entrance to Hop Island and from here until Passage the path runs on a sea-wall embankment along the shoreline of Cork Harbour. It advances due east and then, just before Passage, turns sharply south across the narrow channel from Great Island. Look across the water and you can distinguish the existing railway line to Cobh on the other side of the harbour. The track crosses two sea inlets via stone bridges and then enters the coastal town of Passage through a municipal park. It finally comes to its end in another small park in the centre of Passage town, across the road from a school. This was the site of the original Passage station but hardly a trace remains.

In the last century the town was an important port and the first steamer to cross the Atlantic departed from here, but the town's prosperity has declined in more recent times.

After Passage the railway line continues through a long tunnel to Glenbrook though sadly this tunnel is no longer accessible.

Blarney to Donoughmore

The Cork and Muskerry (C&M) light railway system consisted of a network of small narrow-gauge lines to the north-west of Cork city. The intention behind its construction was the promotion of tourism around Blarney and the improvement of transport links between the city and its hilly, north-western hinterland. The first section to be opened, in 1887, was the line from the Western Road terminus in Cork city to the village of Blarney. The station in Blarney adjoined the grounds of the famous castle. A branch to the village of Coachford, which lies to the east of the city along the River Lee valley, was subsequently built in 1888. The final extension to the system was another branch that left the original Blarney line about 2 km west of the village and ran north-west along the River Shournagh to the isolated village of Donoughmore; it was opened in 1893. The Cork and Muskerry enjoyed its heyday in the years prior to World War I, die to the combination of tourist business to Blarney and its proximity to Cork, Ireland's third largest city. The growing popularity of road transport meant increasing losses and the entire system was closed in 1934.

One walk has been selected from the network, along the Donoughmore branch. It begins close to Blarney village and carries on up the Shournagh river valley between forested hills. As more than sixty years have elapsed since the closure of the line, the track bed is overgrown and the walk is best carried out on the adjacent road. It finishes 1 km east of Donoughmore, at the curiously named hamlet of New Tipperary. Either Cork city or Blarney can be used as a base, both having plentiful accommodation. The C&M station at Blarney, while lacking grandeur, remains intact and stands on the south side of the

village square. It now houses a tourist souvenir shop.
Maps: OS (ROI), Sheet 21 or 25 (half-inch series)

Distance: 14 km.
Time: 2.75 hours.
Start: 2 km west of Blarney, where the River Shournagh crosses the R617 road.
Finish: The small hamlet of New Tipperary.
Description: A pleasant road walk along a river valley through wooded, hilly country.

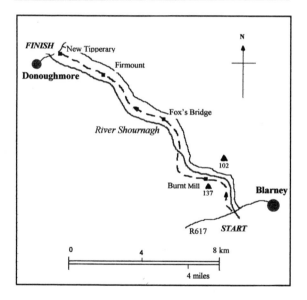

Starting at the road-bridge over the Shournagh river on the R617, follow a small road that runs upstream alongside the river. The road soon enters an enclosed wooded valley, with hazel and ash interspersed with some planted laurel and larch

on the slopes. It curves alongside the river, with the overgrown
railway track running on the opposite bank. After 1.5 km you
reach the site of the first station on the line, Burnt Mill. All
that remains is a ruined building and the skeletal structure of
an old railway girder bridge. There is a makeshift footbridge
over the river here, built from pallets and old rails, which you
can use to inspect the station area on the other side of the
river. Continuing on, it is apparent that rock blasting was
needed to take the road and railway track up the river valley.
In parts, the river is shallow and rocky and noisy and on the
other side of it the track runs along a precarious ledge cut into
the hill. Presently the road takes a sharp right-hand turn,
directly beneath some cliffs, and this marks the end of the
valley stage. From here on, the journey is through rolling
agricultural country. Near this point the railway crosses the
Shournagh and begins to run between the road and the river.
There is no discernible sign of the bridge that must have
existed and the track itself has been invaded by ferns, nettles
and some foxglove. Soon you reach Fox's Bridge station,
which is almost halfway along the route. The station house still
stands, now a private dwelling adjoining a commercial garage at
a crossroads.

Leaving the station, the railway reservation continues to
lie sandwiched between the road and the river. Unfortunately
it is either completely overgrown or ploughed back into fields.
At a former railway-crossing lodge, I met and chatted with the
owner about the railway and he remarked that a local pictorial
history of the branch was about to be produced to celebrate its
centenary, albeit belatedly. Four km after Fox's Bridge, you
come to Firmount station, located at another crossroads. The
attractive station cottage has been extended to form a grocery
shop and it stands beside a pub and hardware stores. You can
just make out the edge of the platform in the lawn of the
station building. There is a pleasant leafy stretch of road after

Firmount and the continuous gentle climb brings you to the edge of the Boggeragh mountains, whose upper slopes appear on the northern horizon. The road, track and river remain in close company and eventually the terminus at New Tipperary is reached. The name has an exciting, pioneering feel though the hamlet itself is an altogether more prosaic spot, with two pubs belligerently facing each other across the road. The pub and house on the left-hand side are on the extensive site of the abandoned station. The village of Donoughmore is 1 km to the west, on top of a steep hill; this explains why the railway did not finish there. New Tipperary was apparently a bustling centre in railway days, with large cattle fairs, but today it feels a little forlorn. There is a once-a-day bus service between it and Cork city.

Waterfall to Bandon

A t the end of the last century, Cork city was served by
five separate railway companies, one of which, the
Cork, Bandon and South Coast Railway (CB&SCR),
was responsible for the rail system to the west and south of the
city. The railway line was established when it was decided to
link Cork with the town of Bandon, 32 km away. This was
accomplished in two stages: the line between Bandon and
Ballinhassig opened in 1849, while the stretch of track which
continued into Cork was completed two years later. The
terminus in Cork was at Albert Quay and the building is still
standing, next to the City Hall. There were a number of
intermediate stations between Cork and Bandon – Waterfall,
Ballinhassig, Crossbarry and Upton – and at Crossbarry there
was also a short branch line down to Kinsale. The system
eventually expanded westwards until it covered almost all
towns in west Cork, including Skibbereen and Bantry. It was
a comprehensive rail system, almost independent from the
rest of the network in Ireland. The railways in this region
remained profitable until World War I but then fell victim
to the widespread pattern of general decline. Service frequency
on the main line was reduced to two trains daily and outlying
branches were shut down. Final closure for the remainder of
the system came in 1961.

The stretch from Cork to Bandon would have made a
very interesting walkway if conversion had taken place soon
after its closure. There are some substantial engineering
features on the line, including the curved ironwork of the
Chetwynd viaduct over the Bandon road, the Gogginshill
tunnel, which is the fourth longest in the country, and the
Inishannon viaduct over the wide Bandon River. Unfortunately,

Waterfall, County Cork

the line passes through intensively farmed land and in many
parts the track has reverted back to agricultural usage, making
a long, continuous walk impractical. Therefore I have selected
two shorter stages which illustrate some of the distinctive

features of the line. The first is from Waterfall, a hamlet situated south-west of Cork, to the village of Halfway, which lies
on the main road from Cork to Bandon (N71). The second
is from the site of Upton station, 6 km west of Halfway, to the
station in Bandon town. Either Cork city or Bandon, an
historic town dating from the Munster plantation, can be
used as a base.

Maps: OS (RoI), Sheet 25 (half-inch series).

STAGE 1: Waterfall to Halfway

> **Distance:** 6 km.
> **Time:** 2.5 hours.
> **Start:** Waterfall village.
> **Finish:** Halfway village on the N71.
> **Description:** A short walk through the hills of South Cork
> including a section in one of Ireland's longest tunnels.

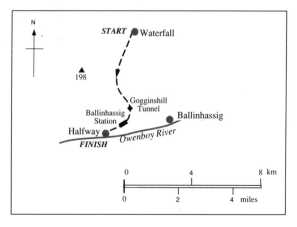

When you enter Waterfall village take the road to the right
at the pub and continue until you reach the large road

underbridge. Waterfall is the first station on the line from Cork and the house on the right is the old station-house. The track can be joined at this point where it runs past a farmhouse on a very tall embankment. There are wonderful views over south Cork from this vantage point. Beyond the farmhouse, the track advances as a long, straight farm lane in a grass cutting with stone mileposts and a row of telegraph poles in the side hedges. This is followed by a short, though sizeable, embankment and then the track levels off and leads into fields. It continues through a deep cutting teeming with brambles and past a partially dismantled stone bridge before crossing the road on a large sandstone rail overbridge. Unfortunately, the track on the bridge is quite overgrown and it is better to join the road for this stretch.

After the bridge the track resumes its path through fields. For the next 1.5 km the ramble is along a valley floor in a deep cutting. This section is rather wet and thorn-infested and it is better to walk through the dairy fields on the right-hand side of the line. There is a series of telegraph poles alongside the cutting, their disconnected cables hanging defeated and forlorn by their sides, and these peter out when the track advances through some scrub. The going becomes easier when a farm trail appears on the track. You then proceed under the remains of a girder footbridge and into Gogginshill tunnel (820 m). The tunnel is the one of the longest in Ireland, only exceeded in length by that on the abandoned Armagh to Newry line and two operational tunnels - one at the entrance to Cork station and the other at Bray on the Wexford line.

The face of Gogginshill tunnel is lined with red brick. The interior walls consist mainly of bare, rough hewn rock though some parts have been lined with masonry. A torch is absolutely essential and if you are walking alone be warned: it is not for the fainthearted! Once inside the tunnel, the entrance and exit openings cannot be seen because the track curves as it runs from a southerly to a westerly direction. There are three circular ventilation shafts along it, each about 3 m in diameter. Looking up through them you can see how deeply the tunnel has been cut. The shafts are reassuring for the rambler, as the periodic injection of a diffuse light means that the entire distance is not covered in implacable darkness. Although water can be heard dripping down from the roof and there are a few puddles of water underfoot, the tunnel has remained predominantly dry. Emerging from it the track passes through a short, overgrown cutting before reaching an unprepossessing building. This is Ballinhassig station, a definite contender for the title of "Most Inaccessible Station"! It is 2 km from the village it was meant to serve and is situated on a high hillside. The lane which led to the station from the village was so steep that it had to be negotiated on foot only: vehicles simply couldn't manage the gradient!

After the station, the track heads due west, running on a ledge that has been cut into the ridge above the Owenboy valley. In parts, it is a farm-track but in other sections the line has been ploughed into fields. The village of Halfway can be seen ahead, sitting astride the road in the valley below. Beyond the large farm shed which has been built on the line is a sturdy, three-arched, stone viaduct which carries the railway over a gorge. After this, the track becomes very cluttered, overgrown and broken, an obvious place to halt the day's walk. A steep cattle path leads down from the viaduct directly into the village. Be sure to look back towards the viaduct – it is all the more impressive when seen in its entirety. There are two pubs in the village and each provide welcome sustenance, though otherwise Halfway is an undistinguished place.

STAGE 2: Upton Station to Bandon

Distance: 8 km.
Time: 3 hours.
Start: Upton station.
Finish: Bandon station.
Description: A walk through wooded river valleys which includes a variety of interesting railway features.

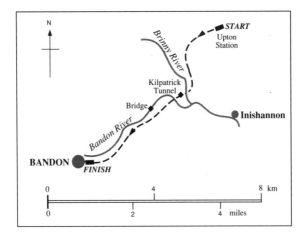

Upton station consists of a large redbrick building with green gable boards, a parcels office and two platforms. It stands at the western end of the Owenboy River valley, 3 km north-west of the town of Inishannon. The station is empty and when I walked the route it was for sale. Apart from a nearby public house, "The Railway Bar", and some derelict cottages, the station does not appear to serve any identifiable population centre. This was not uncommon in the railway network of rural Ireland; many large stations were sited in the most

Upton station, County Cork

remote and seemingly unprofitable of places. The large Celtic Cross in a hedgerow just past the station is a memorial to an incident in the Troubles in the 1920s. The large open fields, rolling hills and mature beech trees are evocative of the South Downs in England, and contributed to the area's popularity in the last century as a location for the country estates of the Anglo-Irish gentry.

Take the road westwards from the station past a housing development and through a crossroads. The railway line ran alongside the left-hand side of the road but this area has now been landscaped into fields. The track can be joined at the first farmhouse on the road, where it runs as a farm lane with telegraph poles along it. You proceed a short distance through the countryside before the track comes across another road, alongside a cream-coloured cottage. This was originally a level-crossing lodge and the man I spoke with there had been a ganger on the West Cork line. His responsibilities had included maintenance of the permanent way and he had many stories about the railway. The track can be rejoined by walking up the approach to the large farm across the road from the cottage, and skirting around the farmyard when you reach the top. It goes through an impressive, long, curved cutting whose sheer rock walls are coated with lime-green moss. The surface underfoot is firm though, as the path is now a stone farm trail. A high embankment carries the track through a deciduous wood and then through another, shorter, curved cutting. Continue on a rock-blasted ledge on the hillside, high above the Brinny River, and then cross the river by a tall, narrow stone bridge. This is a most scenic section, thick with hazel, oak and beech trees – the only unscripted incident in my case being an impromptu diversion to avoid a bull!

On the south side of the Brinny River, the track runs into a deciduous forest and is laden with ferns, leaves and twigs and refreshingly "crunchy" underfoot! An embankment becomes a wide cutting as the Kilpatrick tunnel is approached. It is 150 m long and was the first railway tunnel in Ireland. The stone face and the rock interior are both lined with masonry. Once out of the tunnel, the track continues for a short distance but then comes to an abrupt halt on the large stone pier of the "missing" Inishannon viaduct. There is a super view up- and downstream as the Bandon River winds through a tight, wooded valley. A picnic site can be seen on the other side of the river beside the road to Bandon. Some ingenuity is now required to continue as the river is much too deep and wide to be forded. It is best to climb down the hill to the river bank and walk upstream along the river to a small bridge, about 750 m from the viaduct. After crossing the bridge you can either walk back along the Bandon Road to the picnic site at the viaduct and join the trail just where you left it or expedite matters by joining the track directly across from the bridge.

For the first 2 km from the picnic site towards Bandon the track has been opened as a public walkway and runs as a gravel trail on a ledge excavated into the hillside above the road and river. The valley is covered with a mixture of hardwood trees and there are bright green ferns and rhododendrons in the undergrowth. At the end of the walkway a reasonably comprehensive history of the line is given on display boards. The last 2 km into Bandon are on the hard shoulder and grassy verge of the road because road widening has absorbed the track, though traces of the original railway wall can still be seen in places. The road passes a succession of garage forecourts as it enters Bandon and then the station appears on your left. It is easily identifiable: a long, single-storey redbrick building with a platform in front and a plaque outlining its history on its gable. The station now houses Cork County Council who are responsible for the walkway and appear to have a progressive attitude to the recreational possibilities of abandoned lines within their jurisdiction.

South Kerry

Loo Bridge to Morley's Bridge

The small town of Kenmare is situated at the head of Kenmare Bay in a very scenic part of south Kerry. As with most nineteenth-century towns there were persistent demands that it be included in the rail network, the inhabitants being mindful of the commercial advantages to be secured from such a connection. However, given its isolated location (steamship was the usual means of transport!), the demand for a railway was particularly acute in Kenmare. There were two possible schemes: a branch down from the main Great Southern and Western Railway (GS&WR) line that ran into Killarney, or an extension of the Cork to Macroom line. In the event the former option was selected and the line was completed in 1893. The branch left the main line at Headford Junction, 13 km east of Killarney, ran in a southerly direction to Kilgarvan and then west to Kenmare. There were three intermediate stations on the line: Loo Bridge, Morley's Bridge and Kilgarvan.

At the time, there was criticism that the route chosen ran through some very remote regions, though given the nature of the terrain the GS&WR did not appear to have much choice. However, because it ran through such poorly inhabited areas it was never profitable and was largely dependant on the tourism, fishing and cattle trades. The line had the usual service frequency of three or four trains each day, making connections at Headford. It finally succumbed to economic logic in 1959, the track being lifted in 1960. The main line to Kerry continues to run through Headford Junction although trains no longer stop there. The once busy station has now been reduced to a road level-crossing point. The main line and branch platforms are still there along with the station-master's house and the signal cabin. There is also a monument and headstone marking the spot of an IRA railway ambush that took place here in 1921.

Unfortunately, the majority of the track from Headford Junction to Kenmare has not weathered the years terribly well and so I have selected only one walk, that between the two stations of Loo Bridge and Morley's Bridge. Killarney or Kenmare would prove equally useful as a base for the walk, but I chose Kenmare because of its more direct association with the line. The town is a very pleasing centre. It was an estate town, built according to the plan of the Marquis of Lansdowne in 1775, and consequently there are some impressive limestone buildings and ornate shop fronts. The town now projects itself as an upmarket and cosmopolitan location though there are still plenty of places to eat, drink and sleep at a reasonable price. Sadly, all that remains of the railway station is the redbrick station-master's house, as the site has now been developed into housing areas and a factory. On a more general note, redbrick buildings are not common in the Republic of Ireland and, as they were popular with the rail companies, their existence is a useful guide to an erstwhile railway presence.

Maps: OS (ROI), Sheet 79 (Discovery series, preliminary edition); OS (ROI), Sheet 21 (half-inch series)

Distance: 8.5 km.
Time: 3 hours.
Start: Loo Bridge station on the R569.
Finish: Morley's Bridge.
Description: A walk through mixed woodland on a valley floor, surrounded by low, craggy mountains. The terrain becomes more open as Morley's Bridge is approached.

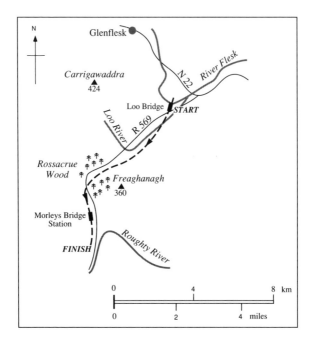

Loo Bridge is 2 km south of the main Cork to Killarney road (N22), and is signposted at the junction outside the hamlet of Glenflesk. Loo Bridge is a townland, the only obvious building in it being the Loo Bridge bar. The station building is just beyond the bar and is now a summer hostel, but the station name board and a railway signal are displayed on the platform to the side of the hostel. There is a girder railway bridge, built in 1892, over the River Flesk just before the station. The owner of the Loo Bridge bar, an amiable man, remarked that a rail enthusiast visiting the area had told him the bridge was the first of its kind in the world, though this is certainly not something which is immediately apparent to the layman.

When the railway track leaves the station, it crosses the road to Kenmare (R569) and then runs alongside that route. However, it is initially overgrown and the rambler is best advised to walk on the road for 200 m and join the track via the meadow on the left. For the first 2 km the track runs close to the Loo River, along the centre of the valley floor and under the gaze of Carrigawaddra Mountain. It is mainly a raised grassy embankment which proves useful as the surrounding fields are wet, covered with reeds and stagnant water pools. Where the track actually crosses the Loo River, the path is overgrown but there is a convenient, parallel farm road that can be taken to avoid this short obstacle. The surrounding, lower slopes of the rugged mountains are heavily planted with mixed woodland which is a refreshing change from the regimented spruce plantations.

As the trail approaches Rossacrue Wood, it becomes lined with silver birch. Indeed, the coating of trees along the trackside is so dense that the grass on the embankment has been replaced by moss. The trees in the birch grove bend together to form a continuous leaf canopy overhanging the trail. This is a beautiful section of the walk: the trees filter the sunlight and cast a distinctive lime-green tint over the earth. A degree of rock blasting was necessary to bring the railway through Rossacrue Wood itself, though the gradients are quite mild. There are two missing bridges over some shallow ponds in the wood but they can be crossed by employing some ingenuity and using the upturned trees that have fallen into the water pools. It strikes me that it is an inexplicable mystery, peculiar to railway walks, why certain bridges have been deliberately taken down when there appears to be no obvious or profitable motive for doing so.

Half-way along the walk, the trail curves around Freaghanagh Mountain on a rocky, ballast-laden ledge and turns due south for Morley's Bridge. The wooded terrain is gradually left behind and the more open landscape offers views of the encircling mountains. There is also an empty gate-lodge at the point where the track crosses to the west side of the Kenmare Road. After briefly running through a small copse, the track continues on its own reservation through some fields. Only the occasional railway sleeper, lying neglected on the ground, reminds the rambler of the forgotten heritage of the area. Hawthorn and willow trees emerge on the embankment, initially quite innocuous but eventually becoming so thick that manoeuvring through the saplings hampers the walker's enjoyment and it is best to walk this last kilometre to Morley's Bridge station on the road through the narrowing valley. The station building is on the right-hand side of the road, a two-storey redbrick building, which is still inhabited as is evidenced by the television satellite dish. The area around Morely's Bridge station was always sparsely populated and would seem to lend substance to the criticism, made at the time of the railway's construction, that the line was never going to be economically viable.

Beyond the station, the track continues as a farm trail running parallel to the road and beneath a cliff-face where a quarry is now in operation. A deserted national school, dating from 1856, is perched on a high stone abutment above the track and it must have been a considerable struggle for the children to climb up the steep path which leads to it. The effort is well repaid, however, as there is a great view of the sharp bend in the Roughty River, where it turns south-west and heads for the sea at Kenmare. Further upstream from the bend you can also see an impressive waterfall. After the school the road has been widened, encroaching on the track until a road-bridge over the Roughty River is reached. This bridge is Morley's Bridge which gave its name to the area. There is a signpost at the bridge for Ireland's highest pub, a title that was recently wrested from a competing venue in the Wicklow Mountains. There is also another monument in the roadside; however at this site, unlike that at Headford Junction, it is the Spanish Civil War and not a domestic conflict that is commemorated.

Glenbeigh to Valentia Harbour

In 1893 a branch line was opened from the main Great
Southern and Western Railway (GS&WR) Tralee line out
to Cahirsiveen on the Iveragh peninsula. A public inquiry
had identified the need of local farmers and fishermen there
for a fast means of transporting their produce to the market
in Britain. The branch line left the main line at Farranfore
and headed westwards through the towns of Castlemaine,
Milltown, Killorglin, Glenbeigh and Cahirsiveen to finish at
Valentia Harbour, across Portmagee Channel from Valentia
Island. Most trains, however, terminated at Cahirsiveen with
only a few continuing on to the small harbour station. The
western part of the line ran through the mountainous terrain
along the south coast of Dingle Bay and is undoubtedly the
most scenic of any of the bygone railway routes in Ireland.

The title of "Most Westerly Railway in Europe" was
hotly contested between this line and the neighbouring
Tralee to Dingle line on the other side of the bay. The title
went to Cahirsiveen, because of its terminus at Valentia
Harbour, although Dingle station was in fact more westerly
than Cahirsiveen station.

Never a profitable route, owing to its remoteness, the railway was closed in 1960 in spite of some intensive lobbying.
Had it survived for a further ten years, the subsequent boom
in tourism in Kerry could have secured its future but, in any
case, the railway's loss is surely the railway rambler's gain!

I have chosen the last 30 km of the line, from Glenbeigh
to Valentia Harbour, for the walk. The route naturally breaks
down into two consecutive stages: Glenbeigh to Kells and
Kells to Valentia Harbour station. The town of Killorglin or
the village of Glenbeigh are equally good bases for the first

section of the walk, while Cahirsiveen is the obvious base for the second stage. Both towns have good bus connections with Killarney and Tralee.

Killorglin is an old-fashioned, somewhat straggly town, though it is lively enough. There is a three-span railway girder bridge over the wide River Laune which has been converted into a short walkway. It affords a magnificent view of the Slieve Mish Mountains on the Dingle Peninsula and to the south of the town you can see the Macgillycuddy Reeks range. Killorglin station-house, notable for its attractive facade, stands on the road to Cahirsiveen and is now being used to house a high-powered international finance centre. Cahirsiveen, while smaller than Killorglin, considers itself to be the capital of the western half of the Iveragh peninsula. Essentially, the town consists of one, very long, winding street and, in spite of its tourist orientation, retains a welcoming and homely feel.

Maps: OS (ROI), Sheets 78 and 83 (Discovery series); OS (ROI), Sheet 20 (half-inch series).

STAGE 1: Glenbeigh to Kells

Distance: 14.5 km.
Time: 5 hours.
Start: Glenbeigh Village.
Finish: Kells Post Office (on the N70).
Description: A magnificent walk in the mountains of the Iveragh peninsula, offering the very best of everything that railway rambling can offer.

Glenbeigh station-house and signal-box can be found on a small road which leads down to the sea. The walk itself commences at the western end of the village where a narrow bridge takes a small road over the River Behy. Turn left after

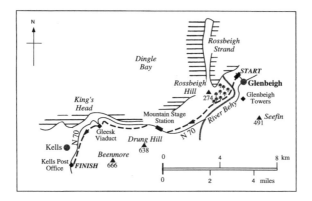

the bridge and 100 m up the road is a dismantled rail bridge, a stone abutment indicating the site. The track proceeds through the forest as a recreational trail with a variety of trees along the side; ash, holly, larch, birch, pine, willow and, especially, oak. Kerry was famous for its oak forests which, sadly, have largely disappeared. The pathway continues along a ledge on the side of Rossbeigh hill and overlooks the Behy River and the Seefin Mountains on the other side of the valley. The huge folly of Glenbeigh Towers, built by a landlord in the last century and burned down in the Civil War, can be seen on the lower slopes of the hills opposite. Presently the forest trail veers off to the right, but the railway track continues on, crossing a small tarred road to become a farm way.

Gradually the track leaves the wooded terrain behind, runs through hilly pasture-land not far from the main road and passes under a sandstone road-bridge. It then curves around the hillside and, while some stretches are fine, others have been ploughed back into fields. Housing begins to appear along the track and eventually progress becomes so slow that it is advisable to rejoin the main road. Because the road here is part of the Ring of Kerry (N70) it is quite busy, with a relentless succession of tour coaches. Stay on it for about 1.5 km at which point you reach a shop on the right-hand side of the road. From here on the N70 actually runs on the widened bed of the railway track through a long cutting, while the original road to Cahirsiveen is off to the left, running parallel to the new road. Take this smaller road, which winds along the slopes of Drung Hill Mountain, until you come to the aptly named Mountain Stage railway station. The station building has survived and is inhabited. It is a two-storey, red building and stands beside a bridge over the widened Cahirsiveen Road. The platform, which can still be made out, lies under a grassy bank down at the level of the new road.

Continuing on, you pass a stone memorial where the original road rejoins the new one. There is a gate-keeper's lodge on the hillside here and beyond this the track runs along a ledge on the heather-coated, northern slopes of Drung Hill. There are superb views over Dingle Bay and the Dingle Peninsula from this vantage point. You can see the long sand spits of Rossbeigh and Inch beaches jutting into the bay and the entrance to Dingle Harbour. The railway ledge, cut into the precipitous slopes of the mountainside, runs high above the road and in parts has become eroded and narrow, so caution should be exercised. Three tunnels are met in quick succession: 50 m, 150 m and 100 m in length respectively, with the latter two being curved. A number of culvert bridges lead the track over some dried-up ravines and then you round a short headland. At this point the Blasket Islands become visible off Slea Head, at the tip of the Dingle Peninsula.

The track widens as it runs through a small forest plantation and carries on along another, more shallow, hill-side ledge. A puzzling concrete maze that turns out to be an extensive sheep-dip must be navigated and then a grassy track brings you to the Gleesk viaduct. This curved, ten-span viaduct, with stone piers and girder sidewalls, is over 30 m tall.

Gleesk Viaduct, County Kerry

It is an excellent example of railway structural architecture, remains in very good condition and is perfectly safe to cross.

For 1.5 km after the viaduct, the going is rather difficult. The track runs on the mountainside as either a cutting or embankment, though parts of it are quite overgrown. The rambler has a choice of either taking the road below or remaining above the track on the open mountainside. The railway curves around King's Head promontory, leaves the sea and heads inland to Kells. If you take the road marked for the hamlet of Kells, the path can be rejoined shortly after a road junction, at a tall rail bridge over a stream. The track is open and clear, making its way either as a ledge or through some slight cuttings on the side of Beenmore Mountain. Picturesque Kells bay, strand and pier can be seen below and beyond them rises the long, ridge mountain of Knocknadobar. There is still plenty of ballast on the track bed and, while there are some missing bridges over narrow streams, the rambler can progress without hindrance. Finally, the track becomes a purpose-built tourist trail meandering behind a large building on the hill which houses Kells Post Office, a restaurant and "craft shop". In spite of its aesthetic short-comings, it is an appropriate point to halt for the day.

STAGE 2: Kells to Valentia Harbour

Distance: 16 km.
Time: 5.25 hours.
Start: Kells Post Office.
Finish: Valentia Harbour station at Reenard Point.
Description: A walk along the mountains and the
  seashore at the western end of the Iveragh peninsula.
Shorter Alternative: Kells to Cahirsiveen (12 km).

Leaving the post office, the track goes through some rocky cuttings as a short tourist trail and then returns to its rougher, natural state. It runs not far from the Cahirsiveen Road advancing along the lower slopes of Been Hill Mountain,

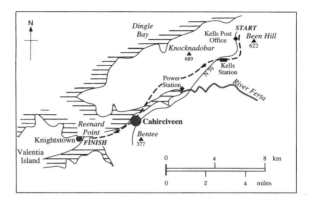

sometimes a little infested with undergrowth. There are numerous small stone bridges over cattle paths and bog streams and a section, colonised for about 200 m by a dense willow thicket, which should be skirted by going through the adjacent fields. On that last point I should say that it is only with the benefit of hindsight that I recommend a diversion – I over-enthusiastically ploughed through it!

The landscape is classic Iveragh Peninsula with the long ridge of Knocknadobar Mountain on the right and, indeed, mountains on every other skyline. The track maintains its altitude as it approaches Kells station, a summit station. After this it drops gradually to sea-level at Cahirsiveen. The title "Kells station" is a geographical misnomer as it is a good two kilometres south of the actual hamlet, something that must have given unfamiliar railway passengers an unwelcome surprise when they arrived at the remote station. The station area is large, encompassing a redbrick station master's house, a signal cabin, a corrugated-iron ticket office and twin plat-forms. The site is empty and, peering into the ticket office, the ticket counter and cashier's hatch can be made out in the dusty gloom.

After the station the railway track crosses to the north side of the road beside two bungalows. For the next 4 km it runs close to the road, through marginal farmland and moor, on the southern slopes of Knocknadobar. The mountain is bare – without a trace of forestry plantation, which is unusual – and the track proceeds mainly as a sheep-grazed embankment. The Ferta river basin spreads out below, with the town of Cahirsiveen visible at its foot. Railway sleepers have been extensively used in the neighbouring fences and are easily identifiable by the tell-tale bolt-holes. In addition the rambler passes a multitude of farm-crossing gates which still bear the engraved GS&WR warnings detailing the penalties incurred if they are left open. Presently the road veers away from the railway track; the former takes a path south of the Valentia River estuary to Cahirsiveen, while the latter goes north of the estuary which it subsequently crosses by a long bridge to reach the town. The hum of cars and coaches fades away to be replaced by the sounds of the cuckoo calling from the moor and the twittering of acrobatic larks. In the midst of all this, the incongruous sight of Cahirsiveen peat-fired power station appears on your left.

The track departs from the mountain-side for the final 3 km as it approaches Cahirsiveen station. It carries on through farmland on the north side of the estuary and, as the hedges and ditches become progressively more difficult to overcome, the rambler might prefer to take the accompanying side-road, lined with willow, fuchsia and gorse hedges. The track crosses this road at a small gate-lodge which still appears to be inhabited. The track bed has now been ploughed under into some lush fields with only a square arched railway bridge surviving to indicate its presence. From the top of this bridge there are panoramic views of the Teermoyle Mountains, Cahirsiveen and Valentia Island beyond, and the Dingle Mountains where they protrude through a gap on the western side of Knocknadobar. After this bridge the best option is to make your way through a meadow down to the shoreline and follow it westwards. Walking on the shoreline is straight-forward even though parts are rocky and covered in seaweed. Then Cahirsiveen, sandwiched between the sea and Bentee Mountain on the opposite shore, comes into view. Once you are around a small headland the long rail bridge appears. It is a spectacular structure, comprising seven main spans nearly 300 m long. The piers of the bridge are stone while its upper works are riveted girders. It crosses the estuary on a diagonal and reaches the other side close to an imposing Disneyesque castle. This, in fact, is an old RIC barracks which is now used as a heritage centre for the town. The bridge is officially regarded as being unsafe (though I crossed it without mishap) and there is a road-bridge less than 200 m away that should be used.

Unfortunately, the station at Cahirsiveen has been com-pletely demolished. It once stood on the waterfront just before the town's quay and, judging by old pictures, it was a substantial building with extensive goods sidings. A hotel was built on the site but that too is gone and has been replaced, rather unromantically, by a sewage works. The end of the walk is 4 km further on, at Reenard Point, but some ramblers may find it more convenient to stop here. Cahirsiveen has an excellent range of places to eat, drink and stay for the night. There are some good examples of old-fashioned country parlour pubs in the town and in one of the more modern and busier pubs – The Fhearta – there is an interesting display of framed cuttings from the *Cork Examiner* which describe the last working day of the line.

For the final section out to Reenard Point the railway track follows the coastline faithfully, passing behind the Valentia weather station. However, it is not in good condi-tion and most of the walk will need to be accomplished on

Bridge near Cahirsiveen, County Kerry

the craggy beach. At Reenard Point there is a derelict, red-brick station-house, all that remains of the Valentia Harbour station. This was the end of the line and passengers for Valentia took a ferry across the channel to Knightstown on the island. The harbour is a tranquil spot, looking out over the sea to Knightstown, and in summer a pub and fish restaurant spring into action – a welcome rest for the hungry rambler.

Lower Camp to Glenagalt Summit

The railway line that once ran between Tralee and Dingle is regarded by many as the most spectacular narrow gauge line in the country. Opened in 1891, it left Tralee at the head of the Dingle Peninsula and fought its way westwards across the Slieve Mish Mountains. For the most part the track followed the path of the main road and had some of the sharpest curves and steepest gradients of any line in Ireland. Due to the unfavourable geography journey times were slow; the 50 km took two hours to complete. As with many of the rural railways, the transport of cattle was a valuable source of income to the company and was given equal importance to the transport of passengers. Despite this, the line was chronically short of finance which meant that the upkeep of the rolling stock and track maintenance were notoriously skimped on. In 1939, passenger services were discontinued as a result of improvements on the Tralee to Dingle road. Thereafter operation was confined to freight but in its last years even this was restricted to a once-a-month service to coincide with Dingle's fair day. This famous line was ultimately closed in the summer of 1953 and the rails were lifted soon after.

Sadly, there is little trace of the railway today. The terminal stations at Tralee and Dingle are gone, although water towers are still present at two intermediate stations: Castlegregory Junction and Anascaul. The impressive Garrynadur viaduct at Lispoole has also survived and can be seen from the road. I have selected a short, central section of the track for a walk which captures the adventure of the line. It is from Lower Camp (the site of Castlegregory Junction station) through the village of Camp with its horseshoe

The original Tralee–Dingle steam locomotive at Blennerville, County Kerry

viaduct and up the ascent to Glenagalt summit. At 207 m, this was the third-highest point recorded on any Irish railway and the long climb up to the top, much of it at a gradient of 1 in 30, was the most gruelling section of railway in the country. However, there are magnificent views over Tralee Bay and the northern side of the Dingle Peninsula all along the way.

The walk starts at Lower Camp, 13 km from Tralee on the road to Dingle (N86). There is a bed-and-breakfast in the nearby village of Camp (1.5 km away) or, alternatively, the walker can use the large town of Tralee as a base and avail of the good bus service to Dingle. Tralee, the county town of Kerry, has plentiful eating and accommodation options, good bus connections and is still on the rail network. Ramblers can also stay in Dingle, which is an extremely lively town in summertime and especially popular with young, continental backpackers.

Another interesting feature of this line is the restored 3 km section from Tralee to Blennerville. The train is powered by an original Tralee and Dingle steam locomotive, although the carriages are Spanish and have been regauged. All the rolling stock has been painted in the livery of the Tralee and Dingle line and it is worth making the journey. Compared to modern rail transport, comfort is quite poor, with much jolting and lurching, and one can only admire the grit and forbearance of those passengers who braved the entire journey to Dingle!

Maps: OS (ROI), Sheet 71 (Discovery series); OS (ROI), Sheet 20 (half-inch series).

Distance: 6.5 km.
Time: 2.5 hours.
Start: Lower Camp (Castlegregory Junction).
Finish: Glenagalt Summit.
Description: A reasonably short walk up a mountain pass.

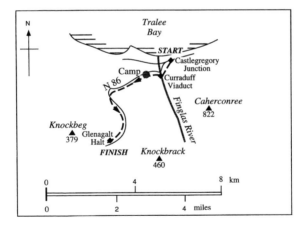

The site of Castlegregory Junction is now a picnic area with parking bays along the left-hand side of the road to Dingle. The station was so named because a short branch line to the village of Castlegregory left the main Dingle line at this point. Only the stone water tower remains with a plaque on it commemorating the railway. There are two pubs across the road. Their names, "The Junction Bar" and "Railway Tavern", reflect their lineage. In literature outlining the history of the line these buildings were wryly described as being part of the station, since the train crews were reputed to adjourn there so often! At the western end of the site is an annular concrete ring, the location of the station's turntable. The scenery is impressive: the large mountain to the west is Stradbally Mountain while the pale-blue Brandon Mountain can be seen peeping out from behind it. Across Tralee Bay is Fenit and beyond that you can discern Kerry Head.

Immediately after the station there is some housing on the line. Walk westwards along the road until it forks, then follow the route to Anascaul and Dingle (N86). An embankment appears on the left and can be accessed across a field. The track carries on over a farm track by means of a partially ruined bridge and continues as a cutting alongside the road. The sharply curved, twin-arched viaduct at Curraduff, just below Camp village, is presently met. This was the site of the worst accident in the history of the Tralee and Dingle line when, in 1893, a train coming down from Dingle at an excessive speed, leapt the rails and plunged into the Finglas River below. To avoid this dangerous, angled viaduct the railway company subsequently diverted the line and built a new bridge over the Finglas River, 300 m upstream. This girder bridge can be seen from the top of the Curraduff viaduct.

For the short distance up to Camp the railway ran to the left of the road, and it is best to stay on the road until the village is reached. The train halted right in front of Ashe's pub and that hostelry, with its low, dark ceiling, still makes a pleasant stop. Leaving Camp the track begins to climb, running on a raised verge along the road. It is mostly overgrown and it is better to use the road. Both road and track head in a westerly direction along the peninsula, with the high peak of Caherconree behind you, and the equally impressive Stradbally before you. At a curve over a stream an original railway bridge can be seen and from this point on the verge is more grassy and can be walked. With the continuous ascent the views become progressively more panoramic over the peninsula. It was on this section, while resting on the heather, that I met a retired farmer who remembered bringing cattle from Annascaul to Camp on the train. He also recounted the, by now familiar, myth about how, when the locomotives were reduced to using wet turf as fuel during the war, they were frequently overtaken by pedestrians on the adjacent road!

Halfway between Camp and the summit, both the road and track turn sharply away from the sea and head southwards into the mountain ridge. The railway line crossed to the other side of the road at this point and the gatekeeper's cottage, now lying empty, is perched up on the hillside. There is a loose stone wall at this curve, built when a train was blown off the track by westerly gales in 1912. For the next 2.5 km the track climbs the mountainside to the pass at Glenagalt. Farmland predominates here and the only obstacles are the barbed wire fences that need to be surmounted. At the summit there is a small station – Glenagalt – and a bridge carrying a by-road over the line. The bridge and station platform remain, although the latter is hidden under a long coating of grass. From the platform, you can see the line curve towards the level-crossing lodge on the corner of the mountain. On the other side of the road-bridge is a deep cutting where trains would stop to be inspected after their arduous ascent. The line continued westwards from here, dropping down through the mountains to Anascaul.

Rathkeale to Templeglantine

etween 1856 and 1880, a line was built to link the city
of Limerick with the town of Tralee in north Kerry. It
ran westwards across County Limerick, through the
towns of Adare, Rathkeale, Newcastle West and Abbeyfeale
and then on into County Kerry. The section between
Rathkeale and Newcastle West was built in 1867 but the
remainder of the line was not finished until 1880. This piece-
meal approach to its construction meant that Newcastle
West was a terminus station and through trains had to reverse
out of it. It also resulted in sections of the line being operated
by separate companies until they eventually amalgamated
into the Great Southern and Western Railway (GS&WR)
in 1901.

In its time the line was a busy provincial railway with four
passenger trains daily to and from Limerick. Operations were
inevitably scaled down as the century wore on and in 1963
passenger services to Tralee were terminated. Freight continued to be carried on sections of the line until the relatively
recent date of 1977 and the line was not formally abandoned
until 1987 when the track was lifted. This makes it the last
major closure on the Irish railway system, although the
eastern end of the line – the branch to Foynes – is still an
operational freight line.

Because the line has only lately been abandoned, it is
unique in that its land not yet been sold back to the farmers.
The Southern Trail Group, based in Newcastle West, hopes
to open it as a recreational trail from the Foynes branch to
the terminus at Tralee. I have chosen a section which will
provide two consecutive day's walking: Rathkeale to Newcastle
West and Newcastle West to Templeglantine. For ramblers

wanting a longer walk, it is possible to continue onwards from Templeglantine to Listowel and then on into Tralee itself. Either Rathkeale or Newcastle West can provide overnight accommodation. Both are attractive towns with some notable historic buildings. They are on the main Limerick to Tralee road (N21) and served by good bus connections.
Map: OS (ROI), Sheet 17 (half-inch series).

STAGE 1: Rathkeale to Newcastle West

Distance: 13 km.
Time: 4.5 hours.
Start: Rathkeale station.
Finish: Newcastle West station.
Description: A walk through the rich, agricultural Golden Vale.
Shorter Alternative: Rathkeale to Ardagh (9 km).

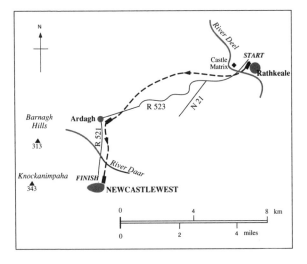

Rathkeale station-house and goods-shed stand close to the roundabout on the new road by-pass. The station-house is built from fine-cut limestone blocks and the perceptive walker may notice its odd orientation with respect to the goods shed. In fact, the station house was moved a short distance, stone-by-stone, from its original location, right beside the roundabout, during construction of the by-pass. The station building now contains the Irish Palatine Heritage Centre which details the history of the settlement of hundreds of German Protestant families in Rathkeale in the early eighteenth century.

When leaving the station, take the small tarmac road to the sewage plant. The railway track, now a gravel path, can be joined at the gates there. It runs alongside the main by-pass road before crossing over the Deal River on a girder bridge and passes Castle Matrix to its right before coming to an end on the main road. You should walk along the road for about 200 m and rejoin the track bed where it emerges on the other side of the road.

The railway runs as a narrow passage between thick green walls of ash and hawthorn hedgerows. As might be expected, considerable amounts of ballast remain on the track and many discarded sleeper bolts are strewn about. The track advances through the rich, fertile and flat plain of central Limerick and as a result there are not many sizeable embankments or cuttings.

Ardagh village lies 7 km ahead, due west. The rambler goes under and over some stone bridges and needs to clamber over trees that have been deliberately felled by farmers to prevent cattle straying on to the line. Through the occasional gaps in the hedges, you can look out over the plain to see the ruins of Anglo-Norman tower houses dotting the countryside.

The second half of the journey to Ardagh is more open, both because the track itself is wider and clearer, and because the hedges are not quite so dense. Eventually the long ridge of hills beyond Newcastle West comes into view. From the top of the last road overbridge, 2.5 km before Ardagh, there is a beautiful view over the Golden Vale – especially glorious on a hazy summer evening.

Shortly after this bridge the going becomes very rough and it is advisable to take the parallel road for 500 m. The track can be rejoined, via a field, just as it curves away from the road. The trail soon runs into Ardagh station on a ballast-laden farm way. The station is in excellent condition: the station-house is still inhabited and there is a parcels office and long platform. Ardagh is a short distance away and is the very model of an Irish village, with an arrangement of pubs and shops strung along a road.

After Ardagh station the track goes under a road-bridge and then curves sharply southwards for the home straight to Newcastle West. This section was apparently cleared some years back by the Southern Trail Group and is quite easy going. The path runs between bramble and willow hedges, narrow in parts, but without any obstacles. It is noticeable that, as the track moves through the less fertile ground at the base of the west Limerick hills, the quality of the neighbouring fields deteriorates. A road is crossed on the level, though there is no sign of any gate lodge, and then the River Daar is crossed by a metal girder and timber beam bridge.

Presently the distinctive twin water towers of Newcastle West hospital protrude on the skyline and the trail passes under a twin-arched road-bridge on the final approach to the station. The incoming line from Rathkeale meets the outgoing line to Tralee at this point. The station area is large and the station buildings, water tower, signal-box, platforms and sidings remain, though they are in poor condition. There is talk that they may be restored, though many such restorations have been discussed around the country without any real action ensuing. There is a new housing development under construction just behind the station and this provides access to Bishop Street in the town. Newcastle West was the capital of the Geraldine earldom and the Desmond Castle in the centre of the town is being restored. There is a very pleasing river walk near the castle and more sociable ramblers will enjoy the lively pubs in the town.

STAGE 2: Newcastle West to Templeglantine

Distance: 13 km.
Time: 4.5 hours.
Start: Newcastle station.
Finish: Templeglantine.
Description: A ramble through the Barnagh Hills with some great views from the summit.
Shorter Alternative: Newcastle West to Barnagh (9 km).

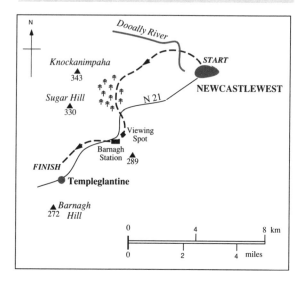

For the first kilometre from Newcastle West station, the track has had gravel chippings laid on it to form a recreational trail. Passing under the twin-arched road-bridge you should take the path to your left at the fork in the track, the Tralee line. The track climbs out of Newcastle West on a curved embankment, followed by a long, slow descent. The gravel path peters out at a level-crossing over a public road and, immediately after this, a river is spanned via a bridge. Thankfully, the vast majority of bridges on the line are still intact, most likely due to its quite recent closure, and they are mainly stone or timber beams and iron girderwork constructions. The track then turns in a large arc on the hillside, changing direction from north to south and continuously gaining height. It runs on an open ballast path between some bramble hedgerows and crosses two small roads in quick succession. The lodges and crossing gates are present at both and I chatted with their respective occupiers about the difficulties involved in having railway lodges as homes. On this section I also met someone who, allegedly following doctor's orders to remedy his back pain, was lying spread-eagled on the uncomfortable ballast enjoying the sun!

The track advances through two long cuttings with an embankment in between. It is a protracted steady climb from the flat Shannon basin up through the Barnagh Hills, and this must have ranked as one of the most prolonged ascents on a major route in the Irish railway system. Beech and sycamore trees join the ash, hawthorn and willow in the fields, while the inevitable plantations of spruce dominate the higher hill slopes. A very tall, stone bridge carries the track over a small road and the trail is a little rough for a while. This difficulty quickly fades and an exhilarating, almost subalpine, section follows as the track courses through the wooded hills on extremely tall embankments. The long bridge that must be crossed high above a cattle path is not exactly in tip-top condition and ramblers must exercise care when crossing. Carrying on through some fuchsia- and foxglove-lined hedges, the track comes out on the main Tralee road (N21). Road widening has removed the track bed along here, so you should clamber down onto the road and walk along it for 150 m to a viewing spot at a corner in the road.

The track can be picked up again near the viewing spot as it crosses a minor road via a stone bridge. It curves sharply westwards on a tall embankment, offering magnificent views over the Limerick plain. On most days the rambler should be able to see the Clare Glens, the smoke of Limerick city with the Silvermine Mountains behind it, and the Galtee Mountains in south Tipperary. The track then plunges into a very deep rock cutting on the approach to Barnagh tunnel. The tunnel, which is about 100 m long and curved, leads to an equally deep but much damper cutting on the other side. Remote Barnagh station with its derelict stone-and-brick station-house lies near the end of the second cutting. The station is the highest point on the line. From here on the track descends through the Barnagh Hills to the town of Abbeyfeale on the Kerry border.

It then runs through a series of shallow, wet cuttings, under a road-bridge and along tall embankments over mountain streams. The landscape here, on a hill plateau, is more exposed and the Tralee Road can be seen across the valley, heading in the same westerly direction as the rail line. A second road-bridge is passed under and the deep, wet cutting that follows may be avoided by taking a brief detour via the neighbouring fields. Continue along the trail until you are opposite the hamlet of Templeglantine. The walk can be terminated here by taking the farm lane to the left of the track into the village, which consists of a few shops clustered around the Devon Hotel. It is also a stopping point for express buses on the Limerick to Tralee route. Alternatively,

Barnagh station, County Limerick

you may decide to carry on a little further: Devon Road station is about 3 km further west, while Abbeyfeale is 8 km away.

Ennistymon to Miltown Malbay

and

Kilkee to Kilrush

The West Clare line has achieved a certain immortality in Irish railway mythology due to the satirical Percy French song, "Are Ye Right There Michael?", detailing its operating peccadilloes. Even if the train kept to its timetable, it took three-and-a-half hours to get from Kilkee to Ennis, a distance of 56 km as the crow flies! Frequently even this proved to be beyond the train's ability, much to the intense irritation of the passengers.

Strictly speaking, the system consisted of two lines, the West Clare Railway and the South Clare Railway. The former ran from Ennis, north to Corofin, west to Ennistymon and then south along the coast through Lahinch and on to Miltown Malbay. The South Clare Railway was an extension from Miltown Malbay down to Kilkee on the Atlantic coast, while a short branch to Kilrush, on the Shannon estuary, left the main line at Moyasta junction.

The narrow gauge railway, built with the intention of opening up the west, was completed in 1892. Despite its reputation, it was one of the more successful narrow gauge railways, carrying 180,000 people in 1910 and servicing the large, monthly cattle fairs at Ennistymon and Miltown Malbay. However, the inexorable decline in the railways made its mark and despite subsequent improvements, such as dieselisation and better service frequency, it was finally closed in 1961. In fact, its demise marked the end of the narrow gauge rail system in Ireland.

Clare's best known natural features are the Burren and Cliffs of Moher, and the railway came close to both, at Ennistymon and Lahinch respectively. Ennis, the large county town with its narrow, winding streets, is a good base for the walk. The town, and indeed the county as a whole, is famous for its love of traditional music. Daniel O'Connell and Eamon de Valera both represented the county at Westminster and are commemorated in the town. At Ennis station, railway history is also on display; the West Clare steam locomotive, *Slieve Callan*, stands on a narrow gauge track under a canopy. The engine is sited where passengers left the mainline Waterford, Limerick and Western Railway platform and boarded the train for Kilkee. The extensive West Clare freight yards, now the site of an ESB depot, were on the other side of the road-bridge at the station.

Rather than walk the whole line, I have selected two stages which conveys its flavour. The first stage commences at Ennistymon and finishes at Miltown Malbay, running on hill ledges and overlooking Liscannor bay. The second is in the flatter south-west area of the county, a walk from the seaside resort of Kilkee to the erstwhile port town of Kilrush. *Maps: OS (ROI), Sheets 57 and 63 (Discovery series), OS (ROI), Sheets 14 and 17 (half-inch series).*

STAGE 1: Ennistymon to Miltown Malbay

Distance: 14.5 km.
Time: 5.5 hours.
Start: Ennistymon station.
Finish: Miltown Malbay station.
Description: A walk on the track bed along the Atlantic coast.
Shorter Alternative: Lahinch to Miltown Malbay (11 km).

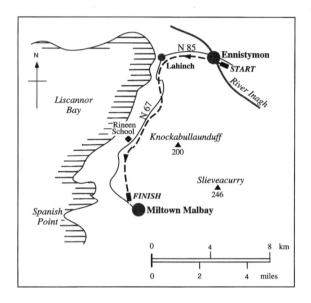

Ennistymon, situated in hilly terrain, is a small market town
with the usual Irish density of pubs and shops. The station is
situated at the outskirts of the town, on the road to Ennis,
and now operates as a bed-and-breakfast. The house itself has
been extensively rebuilt, but an original station shed is still
standing. Walking into town, you can see a rail bridge, constructed of iron girders and stone piers, on the left. Take the
Lahinch Road (N85), which crosses the Inagh River, and
head out of Ennistymon for about 1 km, until the spreading
bungalows peter out. A railway embankment is across a field
on the left and the track can easily be joined at this point.
The track runs along a shelf on the north side of a hill
through shallow embankments and cuttings, parallel to the
Ennistymon to Lahinch road. A certain amount of fencing,
put up by local landowners, must be crossed but it presents no

great obstacle. The country is very open with an almost complete absence of foliage and consists of either bog and moor or else marginal agricultural holdings.

Approaching Lahinch, Liscannor Bay comes into view. The track comes to an end at a T-junction at the outskirts of Lahinch. The railway crossed the road here and the attendant gate-lodge is now a white-washed and extended bungalow. I chatted with the elderly woman who has lived there for over fifty years. She had not altogether fond memories of her chore of closing the crossing gates for oncoming trains. She described the nuisance of late-running trains and the general capriciousness of the line which meant that she could never be sure when to expect a train. I thought her quite unique in not having the prevalent nostalgic affection for old railways and took her testimony to be independent corroboration of Percy French's lament!

Continuing on the back road into Lahinch, you pass through a forest of holiday homes, the development of which has effectively removed Lahinch station. The town of Lahinch is in many ways an archetypal seaside resort, famous for its golfing links and, more recently, its surfing. The beginnings of the Cliffs of Moher can be seen along the north face of the bay. Follow the road to Miltown Malbay (N67) out of the town, past a long caravan park. You should be able to see sections of the track to the left, and 1 km from the town you come to a dismantled railway bridge over the road. The track can be rejoined here by climbing up the stone abutments.

For the next 10 km the track runs on low hills along the shoreline of Liscannor Bay. Initially the route runs in tandem with the coast road and the rambler can avail of the road to avoid some dense undergrowth on the track. The railway, running on a tall embankment where the ballast remains undisturbed, then parts company with the road and approaches a long hill ridge. For the ensuing 2.5 km the path runs along a shelf on the hillside. The way is overgrown and wet in parts, but there is the option of using adjacent fields to avoid the obstacles. I fought my way through and was rewarded for the effort by superb views over Liscannor Bay and out to Hag's Head. A long, dense, elder thicket must be navigated where the trees form a grove on either side of the trail. The walker will come across the foundations of a small building, to the right of the track, which may have been the site of Rineen halt.

The coastal road and railway gradually converge and for another 2.5 km they run alongside. As there are initially quite a few small farms and new houses on the track, it is probably best to use the road for this stretch. Although it can get busy in summer, the road offers picturesque views along the coast. On the seaward side, you pass the distinctive Rineen National School, built of grey brick with ornamental red brick over its doors and windows. Walking up a hill, a stone wall appears on your left and the track can be rejoined here. The path courses through a rock-blasted cutting and at the corner of the hill it runs through a shale quarry. The track then becomes a quarry road passing a railway overbridge that has defied its would-be demolishers and is still standing. The coastal road must be taken again, for 300 m in order to avoid some housing on the track.

For the last stretch to Miltown Malbay the track turns due south, veering away from the road and through open fields along cuttings and embankments; the latter offer views of Mutton Island, off the coast to the south. A number of cattle crossings and small roads with their bridges still intact are crossed and then the white-washed station comes into view at the western edge of Miltown Malbay. Ballast reappears on the track which fords a stream by a tall, culvert bridge. Just before the station, the track passes through a council yard where a platform is visible. Miltown Malbay station has

Former railway bridge near Miltown Malbay, County Clare

also been converted to a bed-and-breakfast though, unfortunately, some rather unsightly chalets have been built across the track linking the original station house with the goods shed opposite. Miltown Malbay is basically one long, wide main street, the northern end of which is dominated by a large Gothic church. Walkers have the option of spending a night in the town or taking a bus back to Ennis or on to Kilkee.

STAGE 2: Kilkee to Kilrush

Distance: 14.5 km.
Time: 5 hours.
Start: Kilkee station.
Finish: Cappa Pier (near Kilrush).
Description: Railway line runs mainly on farm tracks, though sometimes the rambler must use the coastline or adjacent road.

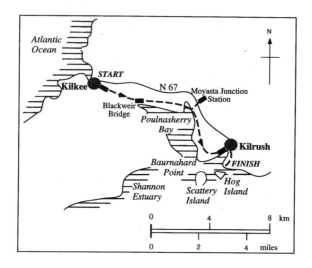

Kilkee is a small, seaside resort with a marvellous beach. The station is at the eastern edge of the town and is dwarfed by a nearby church. The single-storey station building has been converted into apartments and retains its attractive decorative brickwork. More unusually, the platform veranda, with its sturdy cast-iron support columns, has also remained. You can proceed directly from the station across some low-lying fields strewn with rushes, though a certain amount of wire fencing must be negotiated. As with the first stage of this walk, the country is very open, but now the terrain is flat and the forward horizon unbroken. Glancing behind, I felt the landward side of Kilkee looked quite rundown, though perhaps this is the usual appearance of seaside resorts in the off-season.

A gate-lodge guarding a level-crossing over a small road is passed and a shallow embankment brings you to another, identical, gate-lodge. Old sleepers, identifiable by their boltholes, are widely used as fence posting along the track, and a deep cutting carries the track down a low hill and then on to an embankment over swampy ground. This in turn becomes a farm track, meandering alongside the malodorous municipal dump, which provides rich pickings for the many birds. The rambler has to skirt a dense shrub thicket which appears on the path before taking a farm track which leads to the first station of the walk, Blackweir Bridge, almost 5 km from Kilkee. The station-house has been extensively renovated though the platform has been maintained. The eponymous road-bridge is just down on the right and marks the beginning of Poulnasherry Bay, an inlet off the main Shannon estuary. For the next 3 km to Moyasta Junction the line runs along the northern edge of this inlet.

Unfortunately, from Blackweir to Moyasta, the track bed is in poor condition as local farmers have comprehensively reclaimed it, and it is better to walk along the rocky shoreline of Poulnasherry Bay. (Do be careful if walking this route at the start of the year, as the area has very high spring tides.) As you walk along the seaweed-strewn coast, the tall, twin chimneys of Moneypoint power station can be seen to the east together with occasional glimpses of the round tower on Scattery Island. The trail passes two gravel roads leading down to the sea and a ruined house before a sloping stone railway embankment appears on the left. The track can be rejoined at this point, taking you past a farmhouse and on towards Moyasta junction. This is a particularly interesting section as the curved embankment continues on over a stone and girder sea-bridge before terminating at the Kilkee to Kilrush road (N67). There is a pub on the road at Moyasta with the original Moyasta Junction station board displayed outside it. It is owned by Joe Taylor, who has recently published a book by his uncle on a history of the West Clare line. Joe has more ambitious plans to re-open the line from

Kilkee to Kilrush as a narrow gauge summer steam run. The pub makes a fitting venue for any railway rambler to take a break and relax. Moyasta Junction station is just off the main road and up a lane. The two curved platforms for Kilkee and Kilrush-bound trains are in fine condition and the brick station house has recently been repainted.

The track can be picked up again about 100 m from the pub, on the main road to Kilrush. It runs through a field and then as a curved embankment along the shoreline. I encountered a local farmer there and while discussing the line with him, found that he had no objections to its conversion to a steam run or walkway. This is certainly contrary to the popular opinion that farmers are implacably opposed to the re-opening of old railways as recreational facilities.

The trail continues down the east side of Poulnasherry Bay, mainly as a farm track, through poor fields inhabited with windswept, leaning spruce trees. You traverse a short causeway and, at a second level-crossing lodge, the railway begins to turn eastwards, leaving the bay and running along the main Shannon River estuary. Two deep cuttings lead the line along the pebbled coastline of a small sea inlet at Baurnahard Point. Scattery Island with its early Christian settlement lies out in the estuary and closer in to land is the smaller Hog Island, while the dark coast of north Kerry can be seen across the wide river estuary. Presently, Cappa village and its pier come into view straight ahead as the trail approaches Kilrush Creek. The track now becomes routinely interrupted with farm building, cattle and thick hedges as the land improves. At this point, you are only 2.5 km from Kilrush and should take the small road on the left which leads right to the station at the town.

As the road curves into Kilrush Creek it passes two graveyards: the first, Shanakyle, is very old with some elaborate tombs, and many famine victims are buried here. Kilrush station is a long, redbrick building which was originally identical to that at Kilkee. It is sited close to the waterfront at the entrance to Kilrush marina. Two display boards at the entrance to the marina outline the history of the port and the railway.

Kilrush is the second biggest town in the county and styles itself as the unofficial capital of West Clare. It is unusual for the area in that it is a planned town, and, while no longer an active port, the town's architecture retains a nineteenth-century mercantile air. As I half expected, I stumbled across a pub called "The Percy French" in one of the side streets off the square!

For its last kilometre, the track follows the road from Kilrush out to Cappa pier. The line is no longer walkable, though it is worth taking the footpath to Cappa to examine the terminus. The platform and the yard-enclosing walls are at the foot of the sea pier, which is now used as a modest fishing base. There was never a proper station at Cappa; the railway only went out there to connect with boat services from Limerick.

Connemara

Oughterard to Clifden

The western city of Galway acquired a rail service in 1851 under the auspices of the Midland Great Western Railway (MGWR) Company. This was the third largest railway company in Ireland, though it has not been remembered as well as its more famous counterparts, the Great Northern Railway and the Great Southern and Western Railway. Some forty years after reaching Galway, the MGWR decided to extend the line further west, to the Atlantic coast at Clifden. The railway was opened in 1895 and ran from Galway up to Oughterard and then westwards across to Clifden, through Connemara. It had a parallel existence to the Achill branch further north and shared that line's short life span. In fact, the Clifden line closed two years earlier (in 1935) as a result of the unprofitable nature of railway operations in the sparsely populated west. There were three intermediate stations between Oughterard and Clifden: Maam Cross, Recess and Ballynahinch. At Recess the company built a hotel beside the station in an attempt to encourage and profit by tourism.

The station at Oughterard is a large, imposing, grey stone building and is situated 1 km outside the town, on the road to Costelloe. Illustrating the heterogeneity of roles that old stations now fulfil, this particular one is now part of a carpet factory! Regrettably the village of Oughterard, which primarily serves as a fishing base for Lough Corrib, cannot match its station for interest. For those ramblers with transport, Galway city would certainly be a better point from which to undertake the first section of the walk. One logistical drawback of this route is that the intervening country between Oughterard and Clifden is devoid of villages, with the exception of the

Oughterard station, County Galway

tiny hamlet of Recess. For this reason the last two sections of the walk are best tackled from Clifden, "the Capital of Connemara", a small, but lively market town with all the facilities that a rambler could require. Advance booking might be wise though as the town can get very busy at the height of the summer.

The distance from Oughterard to Clifden is slightly over 48 km. As the track close to Oughterard is overgrown in parts, I suggest starting 6.5 km west of the town. For a large part, the walk maintains quite close company with the Oughterard to Clifden road (N59), and the track has remained in a uniformly walkable condition, putting very few physical obstacles in the way of the rambler. The first stage is from The Quiet Man bridge to a point 6.5 km west of Maam Cross. It brings the walker through the open moorland of the area known as *Iar Connacht*, under the shadow of the Maam Turk Mountains. The second stage continues on from this point along the southern edges of the Twelve Pins mountain range, finishing at Ballynahinch station. The final stage is from Ballynahinch to the railway terminus at Clifden, situated on the Atlantic fringe.

Maps: OS (ROI), Sheets 44 and 45 (Discovery series); OS (ROI), Sheet 10, (half-inch series).

STAGE 1: Oughterard to Lough Oorid

Distance: 15 km.
Time: 4.5 hours.
Start: The Quiet Man bridge, west of Oughterard.
Finish: On the N59 beside Lough Shannaghcloontippen.
Description: An uninterrupted walk across moorland below the Maam Turk Mountains.

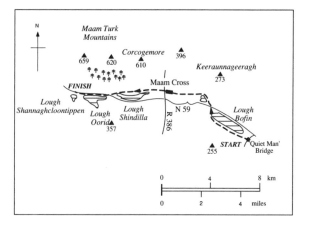

Take the N59 west out of Oughterard. The remains of the railway line can be seen, south of the road, running in the same westerly direction. A signpost for The Quiet Man bridge, 6 km from Oughterard on the left of the road, marks the starting point of the walk, and the stone bridge itself is only 150 m off the main road. The bridge was given its name because it featured in John Ford's classic film, *The Quiet Man*, which was shot in this area. Beyond the bridge, the road forks and the small tarred road to the right is built on the original track bed. It is little-used nowadays, serving only a few isolated farmhouses along the south shore of Lough Bofin. The surrounding terrain is made up of the usual western small-holdings, although the hedges on the roadside are well vegetated with horse chestnut, holly, hawthorn and spruce trees. Halfway along the trail the tarred road is replaced by a rougher gravel road and the countryside becomes wilder and more barren. The track runs on a curved embankment and swings around the end of the lake, heading for a forest plantation. A stone and girder bridge carries the embankment over a river. Its architectural appeal has, unfortunately, been diminished by the addition of concrete breeze blocks to its corners. The track skirts the forest, then approaches and crosses the main road as a shallow cutting in the bog. A cottage stands at the intersection and must have been a level-crossing gate-lodge when the railway was in operation.

North of the road the path runs on a luxurious grassy embankment followed by a cutting that reveals the native red sandstone of the region. The track becomes a gravel road which climbs up past a small lake and over some brown bog streams. The line peaks and turns sharply west, heading directly for Maam Cross, 3 km away on the horizon. The bog is wide and open with the occasional gorse and willow cluster providing scant shelter from the elements. A short distance to the north, the Maam Turk Mountains rise steeply up from the plateau floor, devoid of foothills. Some dilapidated turf storage-sheds and derelict turf-cutting machinery have been abandoned on the moor.

Maam Cross station, 9 km from the start of the walk, is quickly reached and comprises a station-house, goods-shed, water tower and twin platforms. Passengers waiting for the train would have had ample warning of its impending arrival, seeing the steam billowing from the locomotive at a great distance across the barren moor. It never fails to intrigue me that even in the most unpopulated of regions, the railway companies always felt it imperative to build grandiose stations. Sadly, the station complex is derelict and it now adjoins an unsightly cattle mart. The nearby hamlet of Maam Cross contains a shop, restaurant and hostel.

When you leave the station, cross the road to Leenane where the line continues as a farm track. The scenery improves as the desolation of *Iar Connacht* blends into the more rounded terrain of Connemara. The track runs along the north shoreline of Lough Shindilla as a bog road on a series of cuttings and embankments, right under the southern slopes of the Maam Turk mountains. There is a band of dark-green, spruce forest along the base of the mountain range while, across the water on the opposite shoreline, is a lighter, mixed deciduous wood. A fast-flowing river is crossed by a stone and girder bridge and then a long, 6 m-deep rock cutting hauls the track up a rise and crosses the main road again. The trail now runs between the road and the northern shore of Lough Oorid. For a stretch, the track bed has become the base for a new road to Clifden and it is easier to stroll along the old road, beside it. Apart from the sound of traffic on the road, it is a serene and peaceful walk, a few lonely homesteads breaking the expanse of mountain and moor.

The path leaves Lough Oorid, firstly as a cutting in the bog, and then as an embankment along a road behind some houses. This is the only remotely difficult section, with some fencing, blackberry brambles and hawthorn to be negotiated. There is a bridge missing over a stream, a rare occurrence on this line, but it presents no major problem. The grass embankment continues over another river. Shortly further on, the small, though substantially-named, Lough Shannaghcloontippen, seemed to mark a fitting end to the day's voyage.

STAGE 2: Lough Oorid to Ballynahinch

Distance: 14.5 km.

Time: 6 hours.

Start: On the N59 beside Lough Shannaghcloontippen.

Finish: Ballynahinch Station on the R341.

Description: A varied walk through moor and woodland along the south face of the Twelve Pins mountain range.

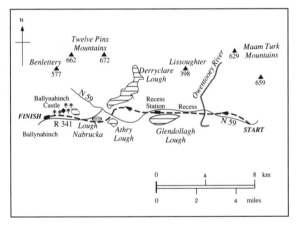

Take the small road westwards that runs parallel to the N59. This was the original road to Clifden and the new main road now runs on the path of the railway track. However, the small road offers a more enjoyable walk. After a gentle descent into a valley, the main road can be seen curving away through a cutting and down a long hill ledge. The Maam Turks begin to peel away to the north-west and the Twelve Pins mountain range comes into view. About 2.5 km from the start, the small road rejoins the main road and the railway track returns to the bog on your left. It becomes an animal trail, running parallel with the road, and then enters a deep cutting, lined with crooked, windswept trees. The walker should take the road beyond the cutting as, further on, the railway bridge over the Owentooey River has been removed. The river is too wide to be forded and the adjacent road bridge must be taken to cross it. Remain on the road until you come to a church, notable for its Spanish mission-style architecture, and then rejoin the railway track.

There is now a good stretch on a dry embankment, with a footpath through some furze-lined parts. The embankment proceeds alongside a tributary of the Owentooey River and comes to an end at a cutting over 20 m deep. Cuttings of this magnitude rarely dry out properly, and it is necessary to return to the road. The line can be picked up again at a corrugated shed further along the trail at the start of scenic Glendollagh Lough. The embankment carries on between the road and the lake shore and then runs on the hard shoulder of the road as it approaches Recess, 6.5 km from the start of the walk. Recess is simply a single row of shops and a pub, one of the shops advertising itself as a retail point for the eclectic mixture of "beer, books, eggs, marble, wool"! Beyond Recess, the track veers away from the road to run on its own causeway reservation in the lake. Although access to it is overgrown, it is worth persevering because once you are on the reservation the going is easy. Some insignificant rock cuttings are traversed before the track reaches Recess station on a gravel road. The station lies at the western end of Glendollagh Lough and has its own wooded shelter belt. It is a single-storey, stone building which has been converted into apartments with somewhat out-of-character patios at the front and rear. The larger building on the other side of the station is the original railway hotel and is still operational.

A girder bridge carries the track over a river joining Glendollagh Lough with its larger neighbour, Derryclare Lough. The line crosses the main road at a right angle and then heads off into open country behind a house on the road. This is a superb section. Away from the road the track runs on a grass embankment along the south shore of Derryclare Lough with the Twelve Pins rising up from the opposite shoreline. A dense spruce plantation marks the left flank and the trail becomes a bog road, re-crossing the main road, again at right angles. This is the last of its many intersections with the N59 and a derelict gate-lodge guards the level crossing, 9.5 km from the start of the walk. The trail continues along the western side of Athry Lough, where the construction of the track required extensive rock blasting. It then curves around on a tall embankment to align itself with the southern shoreline of Lough Nabrucka. There is a missing river bridge on the embankment, but stones have been considerably placed in the river to facilitate its crossing. The path runs on a gravel-topped ledge above Lough Nabrucka and then becomes a tarred road, passing a graveyard on the left and then going through an impressively deep, curved, rock-walled cutting.

The track advances in the form of an embankment and meets the R341 to Roundstone. Part of the embankment has been torn down to make way for a house and stable and the road must be taken for a short duration. The track can be found again at a level-crossing lodge, easily identifiable by its red brickwork and two scrawny, monkey-puzzle trees in its garden. A shallow embankment is lined with a silver birch copse and the track carries on past a small lake. This is another marvellous stretch, offering a great vista of the looming southern face of the Twelve Pins. The deciduous wood is followed by a planted sitka spruce forest in which the track is employed as a forestry road. These dense plantations

Ballynahinch station, County Galway

retain dampness and hence the bed of the track is coated with a thick, luxurious carpet of moss. In turn the spruce forest gives way to a mixed woodland of larch, holly, birch, sycamore and rhododendron. The path becomes indistinct as it nears Ballynahinch Castle and the adjacent road, only 10 m away, offers an alternative route. At the castle, it runs between the main gates and the lodge, which must have made for a very convenient station for the castle's inhabitants!

For the last kilometre to Ballynahinch station itself the track runs beside another lake. However, it becomes impassable and on this occasion the culprits are not the usual bramble and gorse but fallen tree stumps and dense shrubbery, especially rhododendron. Once again it is advisable to take the road until the station is reached. This is a two-storey, redbrick building with a platform veranda overhanging the track and is now maintained as a mountain tourist lodge.

There is a stunning view from a platform area over a nearby lake to mixed woodland on the far shore and the backdrop of the Connemara mountains. Even more so than Maam Cross, Ballynahinch is a perfect example of a finely crafted, expensive station built without any discernable population or hinterland to serve. I don't want to end this walk on a sourly quizzical note, but must say that it seems hardly surprising to me that the railway company ran into financial difficulties with this particular line!

STAGE 3: Ballynahinch to Clifden

Distance: 11 km.
Time: 3.5 hours.
Start: Ballynahinch station.
Finish: Clifden station.
Description: A shorter walk than the previous one, initially on a track through the moor, then dropping down a valley into Clifden.

A large girder bridge carries the track over the Ballynahinch River immediately after the station. A stile at the end of the bridge provides access to the footpath on the embankment, which runs through a small pine plantation. A gravel path takes the line up a long, sloping cutting and the track then levels out in wild, open moorland. The moor is rocky and undulating, unlike the bog at Maam Cross, and is covered with a mixed coating of heather, gorse, rushes and grass. The next 5 km are possibly the loneliest section of the entire walk with not a trace of human habitation or cultivation visible.

The track, functioning as a forestry road, runs through a young spruce plantation. There are innumerable small lakes on either side of the path and many culvert bridges over streams connecting them. The day I walked this section, the

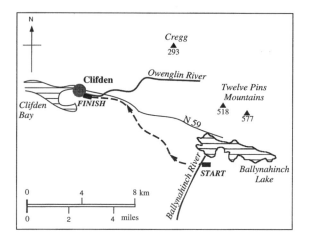

sky was a sullen grey and the cloud ceiling was down to 150 m, obscuring the Twelve Pins. A large bridge over a river denotes the end of the forestry and the track enters a long, leftwards curve through a series of cuttings blasted in rock outcroppings. Many of the rocks are hidden under a layer of white lichen and on the track bed the occasional piece of Connemara marble indicates the complex geology of this region.

The television transmitter at Clifden punctures the western skyline and can act as a visual navigation aid, though the going is so straightforward that its assistance is hardly necessary. The track, guarded by loose stone walls on either side, straightens out and then runs, straight as an arrow, in a north-westerly direction. Sheep farming, turf cutting and housing reappear as the trail passes another pine plantation, its border leavened by the addition of larch and ash. The track crosses a small tarred road where a gate lodge stands, and then a sharply curving embankment carries it along a side road to the main Clifden Road (N59). A distance of 8 km has been covered, though it scarcely feels like it as the walking on gravel bog roads is so free.

At the main road, there is a rail bridge under a short stretch of the original Clifden road. Beyond this the track falls away down a deep, wet cutting towards the town. Stay on the main road as the line is overgrown with willow and silver birch. Just before the bridge over the Owenglin River the track, now on your right, can be rejoined. It runs on an embankment and along a hill ledge, then falls steadily to the station. The twin steeples of the Catholic and Anglican churches can be seen ahead but the eastern approaches to the town are not impressive, spoiled by the delapidated sheds of another cattle mart. The track passes under a cliff face and comes to an end at a dismantled bridge over the Owenglin. You can actually see the water tower at the station from here, but you must take the adjoining road to complete the journey.

Clifden is only half a mile away and the road is pleasant, with fuchsia- and lilac-lined hedges. Clifden station is a two-storey, redbrick building with matching red tiles on the roof and platform veranda intact. There is a stone water tower with a metal tank on top and a redbrick locomotive maintenance shed. The station lies empty and unused, which seems a pity as it would add considerably to the town's charm if it were restored. Clifden is definitely a tourist centre, with a summer vigour characteristic of the busy west coast towns.

Westport to Achill Sound

This line was one of two westerly extensions to the Atlantic coast by the Midland Great Western Railway (MGWR) Company (the other line being from Galway City to Clifden). From Westport the railway extended north to the village of Newport and then westwards, along Clew Bay, to Mullaranny. It continued from Mullaranny through the Corraun peninsula and terminated at Achill Sound, across a narrow stretch of water from Achill Island. There were stations at Newport, Mullaranny and Achill Sound. The line was built in 1894-5 and had the usual service of three trains each way, daily except Sunday. Running through the sparsely populated western coastline, it was never financially successful and was closed in 1937. The line is chillingly famous for the prediction of a local man that the first and last trains to run on it would carry coffins. This indeed proved to be the case: the first train to run carried the coffins of several Achill Islanders back to the island – they had drowned when their boat capsized outside Westport Harbour in 1895. The last train before closure also carried the bodies of men from the island – they had been killed in a mining disaster in Scotland and were being returned to Achill Island for burial.

The base for the walk is Westport, a unusual town because it is one of the few planned towns in the west of Ireland. It was laid out in the eighteenth century under the direction of the Altamount family, who were the major landlords. Although undeniably a tourist town and very busy in the summer season, it retains an air of unspoiled elegance and charm. It has good bus and rail connections with the rest of the country and ample accommodation and places to eat.

There are also some great pubs in the town. Newport is considerably smaller and, while overlooked by most tourists, is a pleasant stopover. Mullaranny and Achill Sound are hamlets, though they possess a selection of accommodation and food outlets. There is a fair local bus service from Westport to Achill Island, passing through Newport and Mullaranny, which can also be utilised by walkers.

I have selected three stages for walking. The first stage is not actually part of the Westport to Achill line. It is along a short spur of track built to connect Westport town with its harbour. This spur was closed some years back by Irish Rail and is now a recreational walkway. On the main walk, I have omitted the first stretch of line from Westport to Newport as sections of it have been broken up and the scenery cannot match the views which prevail further west. The remainder of the line has been divided into two walks: from Newport to Mullaranny and from there on to Achill Sound. The first section is along the mountain slopes on the north side of Clew Bay. The stage from Mullaranny to Achill Sound is mostly in the Corraun peninsula, running through moorland along the coastline.

Maps: OS (ROI), Sheets 30 and 31 (Discovery series); OS (ROI), Sheets 6 and 10 (half-inch series).

STAGE 1: Westport to Westport Quay

Distance: 3 km.
Time: 0.75 hours.
Start: Top of High Street.
Finish: Westport Quay.
Description: Short purpose-built walkway.

From the clock tower at the centre of town, walk up the short, steep High Street to a road-bridge over the railway. In the wall beside the bridge a stile leads down to the gravel track. This pathway out to the quay was opened in 1995 and is a rare example in Ireland of the conversion of a railway track to walkway. The track falls steadily from the town down to the harbour, passing through two rock-blasted cuttings and over a long embankment. The only other engineering feature of note is a second road overbridge. Tremendous views of Croagh Patrick, with its distinctive sugar-loaf profile, can be had along the path. Towards the end the track curves to the right and finishes by running alongside a newly-built school. This was the site of the old station which was pulled down in the late 1980s. Lately there has been frenetic housing development in this area, and a little imagination is required to discern how the railway would have run through this stretch, crossing the road where a beer garden now stands, and continuing right out to the waterfront. At one stage the quayside was a busy port, serving the entire county of Mayo and, as late as the 1960s, ships carrying coal and other bulk goods pulled up here and transferred their cargo to the trains. Westport Harbour is now regarded as an exclusive residential area and has a number of fine stone warehouses. In the evening, there is a great sense of tranquillity in the place with the crowds departed and the sun, setting behind Croagh Patrick, casting long shadows over island-spangled Clew Bay.

STAGE 2: Newport to Mullaranny

Distance: 18 km.
Time: 6.5 hours.
Start: Newport village.
Finish: Mullaranny village.
Description: A long walk, initially through low-lying country, but getting increasingly mountainous, with the scenery improving correspondingly.
Shorter Alternative: Burrishole to Mullaranny (15 km).

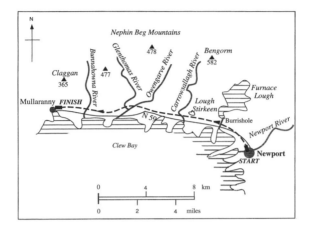

Although it has been almost sixty years since Newport lost the railway, the heritage of its construction still dominates the area. A stone-faced tunnel brought the track through hills south of the town and then a tall embankment and a seven-arched viaduct carried it over the Newport River and into the station. The viaduct was built from local red sandstone, as indeed most of the line's architecture was, and is attractively floodlit at night. The track bed on the viaduct has been transformed into a linear park with flower beds and benches. There are great views: upstream along the wooded Newport River and downstream to Newport Quay on the estuary.

The station at Newport, situated behind the main street, can be reached up an alleyway beside a car showroom. The station-house is inhabited and, as with all stations, appears an attractive residence. However, as one of its tenant's confirmed, the tall ceilings and large single-glazed windows can make for cold winters. The nearby parcel office is now a Catholic oratory. The whole station area is actually in a cutting and an original iron girder bridge carries a road over it.

Take the N59 road to Achill. For the first 3 km, to Burrishole, the track runs beside the road and, in parts, the track has actually been taken over by the enlarged road. A number of rail bridges over and under small side roads are passed. The road-bridge over Burrishole Channel, which drains Furnace Lough into Newport Bay, is in fact built on the remains of the original railway bridge. Immediately after this bridge, follow the small road to the right and the railway track, now running away from the road, can be picked up at a dismantled bridge. The track carries on along the southern shore of Furnace Lough as a wooded embankment. In parts, it may be overgrown with hawthorn and holly trees and the walker can use the nearby parallel lough shore. The trail proceeds through some poor agricultural land, mainly populated by sheep, though interspersed with some dairy cattle. It exists as a close cropped low embankment crossing a number of small tarred roads that lead up to the mountains. A mile on, you pass Lough Stirkeen and the track begins to run on the open, heather-covered slopes of the Nephin Beg mountain range. A long embankment draws the line up an incline and you go under a stone road-bridge at the summit. After the summit two dismantled bridges, over the Carrowsallagh river and another mountain stream, must be overcome. The rivers are fast, shallow and very rocky, enabling them to be easily forded, at least in summertime! The unmistakable outline of Croagh Patrick can be seen across Clew Bay and Corraun Mountain lies straight ahead, with the track drawing ever closer to it.

The line now approaches the main road and returns to a more agricultural domain. Willow and hazel trees reappear in the hedges as do sheep in the fields. Sheep can at times be a nuisance to the rambler with their unerring instinct to let themselves be unintentionally herded. However, on balance they are a railway walker's friend as their intensive and undiscriminating grazing keeps track infestation to a minimum.

In parts, the way is swampy and it is necessary to stray into neighbouring fields. More bridges leading minor roads up to the mountain are passed under and eventually the track moves back on to the mountain. If the day is fine this is an excellent spot to enjoy of an al fresco lunch!

The remaining 8 km into Mullaranny along the mountainside is one of the best railway walks in the country. The foreground scenery is typical west-of-Ireland mountain terrain, while across Clew Bay the Sheeffry Mountains behind Croagh Patrick demarcate the southern skyline. The archipelago guarding the entries to Westport and Newport harbours can be seen at the eastern end of Clew Bay. Out west, further out to sea, lie Clare Island, Inishturk and Inishbofin. A dismantled bridge over the Owengarve River must be negotiated, which may involve removing your boots and gingerly tip-toeing across its rocky bed. A long, curving embankment threads the line through the foothills of the Nephin Beg mountains, with the Owengarve now flowing below. A second, this time intact, bridge takes you over the Glenthomas River and then a series of cuttings, farm and bog tracks haul the line up a continuous incline to a summit with a perfect view.

The track continues along the mountain side on a gravel road to a summer cottage. After the cottage it becomes a track through a rhododendron and larch copse and then a tall, single-arched, sandstone bridge carries it high over the Bunnahowna River gorge. A shallow cutting with loose stone walls on either side marks the point at which the railway starts to lose height and descends to Mullarany. The track is open at first but then becomes a narrow footpath winding through some heavy gorse infestation. Mullaranny village and beach come into view and a farm track brings the trail alongside and above the main village road. Skirting a house which has been built on the track, you will then come upon a railway building that now functions as the local parish hall. The station is just beyond this and is a large, impressive building. It is two-storeys high, built entirely of redbrick, with an attractive waiting room and water tower opposite. It lies empty and unused but the exterior is in remarkably good condition, given that it was closed in 1937. The whole station area is nicely landscaped with the warm lush vegetation that thrives around Mullaranny. It is very reminiscent of south-west Cork with fuchsias and rhododendrons in the hedges. The village itself is of more limited appeal and serves as a tourist stop-over on the road to Achill.

STAGE 3: Mullaranny to Achill Sound

Distance: 14 km.
Time: 5 hours.
Start: Mullaranny station.
Finish: Achill Sound station on the western side of the Corraun peninsula.
Description: An easy walk, for the most part on gravel roads, through open moorland.

Mullaranny station is just off the main road at a small junction signposted for the parish hall. From the station, the line runs behind the railway hotel and through coniferous forestry that has been gently lightened with some larch and birch. Two cuttings bring the track through the western end of the Nephin Beg mountains and a bridge carries it over the main road (N59) and on to the Corraun peninsula. The next section can only be described as idyllic: the path runs along a steep hill ledge and embankment over the southern shore of Bellacragher Bay, passing between a long silver birch wood with purple heather underfoot and through some rocky cuttings with a luxurious lime-green moss cover.

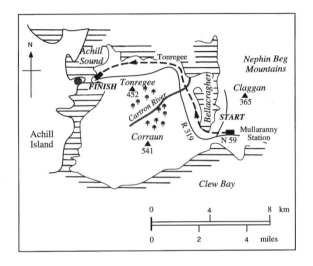

The track joins the road and runs alongside it for a short section, inside an enclosure of two, loose stone walls. It is reasonably overgrown with gorse and you may wish to proceed on the road instead. The track then veers away as an open grass embankment and evolves into a gravel turfcutters' road through the bog along the western rocky side of Bellacragher Bay. For 5 km it travels in a northerly direction past the two mountain masses on the peninsula, Corraun in the south and Tonregee in the north. With the exception of a large forestry plantation in the valley between the two mountains, the eastern side of the peninsula is bare and open moorland. Two brothers were out cutting turf, their black Morris Minor ticking over beside them. They proved to be quite knowledgeable about the line and when I explained my purpose the elder of the two remarked that he had been on the train from Mullaranny to Westport before the war. He mentioned that there had been some talk in the recent past of reopening the railway as a summer steam run but it faded when it became clear that the costs involved would be prohibitive. Walking up the peninsula, the north face of the Nephin Beg mountains and the high peak of Glennamong become visible. The shallow Cartron River must be crossed as the bridge is down and the track then resumes as an embankment, again between parallel stone walls.

The railway rejoins the road and both turn west for the second-half of the route to Achill Sound. For slightly over 1 km, at the dispersed hamlet of Tonregee, the track is broken up by housing, gardens and fields, and the road can provide a more direct alternative. The track then veers away from the road and, for the last 5 km to the terminus, runs along the north coast of the Corraun peninsula under the falling slopes of Tonregee Mountain.

Walking this section is fast and easy, as the trail is predominantly a raised gravel road over the moor, punctuated by shorter, wetter sections through shallow bog cuttings. Deep cuttings in a bog are invariably heavily waterlogged as they lie below the surrounding water level, but happily this is not a problem here. There is considerably more housing on the north side of the peninsula compared to the empty eastern region. Curiously, a number of the houses have flat roofs which hardly seems sensible in this rain-prone land. The terrain is very open and exposed, with the forward skyline only broken by the mountains on Achill Island. As seems to be customary by now, some small culverts over bog drainage streams have been removed, but crossing them presents no challenge.

Presently the railway descends to Achill Sound and Achill Island can be seen across the water. The last kilometre into the station begins deceptively easily, with ballast on the track. However, it quickly drops into a deep, waterlogged cutting with impenetrable, prickly gorse on either side. It is best to skirt this obstruction by walking over the bog on the seaward side. You can then walk along the untidy shoreline and straight into the station beside the quay. Once again it is an extensive establishment with a station-house, parcel office, water tower, platforms and sidings. The house itself is a two-storey, stone building with redbrick at its corners and over the windows. It now acts as a hostel during the summer, which should prove very suitable for some ramblers. The main village at Achill Sound is larger than Mullaranny and is situated across the bridge, on the island.

Florencecourt to Cornacloy

The line which ran from Enniskillen to Sligo, passing through the counties of Fermanagh, Cavan, Leitrim and Sligo, was in many respects unique. The railway was completed in 1882 and throughout its life was operated by the Sligo Leitrim and Northern Counties Railway (SL&NCR) Company. Unlike most other small rural lines it was never absorbed by its larger competitors. At Enniskillen and Sligo it made connections with the Great Northern and Great Southern Railway Companies respectively and, in fact, the line's primary purpose was as a rail link between these two systems. Running, as it did, through a sparsely populated region, revenue was never large and business was not helped by the subsequent establishment of the Border in 1922, which split the railway's operation between Northern Ireland and the Republic. The decision in 1957 by the authorities in the North to close the main line to Enniskillen effectively sounded the death knell for the SL&NCR. With through services from Enniskillen now rendered impossible, its *raison d'etre* was removed and it too shut in that same year.

The site of Enniskillen station is situated on a low hill at the eastern end of the town, across from the Dunnes Stores supermarket. Some stone warehouses still stand there and now house various small businesses. The stone piers of a large bridge that carried the line over the River Erne can be seen just outside the town on the road to Belfast.

Manorhamilton, County Leitrim, was the headquarters of the line and the large station there remains intact, standing outside the town on the Enniskillen Road. I have chosen two consecutive stages from this railway line for walking: Florencecourt station to Belcoo, and Belcoo to a point 8 km

outside Manorhamilton. This is an area of understated beauty
with low mountains and a multitude of lakes. Enniskillen, a
large attractive town with frequent bus services to Belfast,
makes a good eastern base for the walk. The twin villages of
Belcoo and Blacklion, the former in County Fermanagh and
the latter just across the border in County Cavan, lie close to
the centre of the walk and offer more limited eating and
accommodation facilities. Manorhamilton, at the western
end, can also be used as a base. Between Enniskillen and
Manorhamilton the track follows closely the course of the
main road although from Manorhamilton onwards their paths
diverge. Hence walkers may use the bus service between
Enniskillen and Sligo to get to each stage of the walk.

Maps: OS (NI), Sheet 26; OS (ROI), Sheet 7, (half-inch series).

STAGE 1: Florencecourt Station to Belcoo

Distance: 11 km.
Time: 3.25 hours.
Start: Florencecourt station.
Finish: Belcoo station.
Description: Walking on a small public road and along the
northern shoreline of Lough Macnean Lower to Belcoo.

Florencecourt station can be reached by taking the road
from Enniskillen to Sligo. At the crossroads 8 km out from
Enniskillen (just before the hamlet of Letterbreen), take the
road to the left, signposted Florencecourt House. The station-
house is 1 km down this road on the left-hand side. The building
is inhabited and the station area includes twin platforms and
a goods shed. For the first 6 km the track runs on a peaceful,
tarred road on a low embankment through hilly pasture,
following the Arney river basin as it flows towards Lough
Macnean Lower. On your left are squat low hills sitting

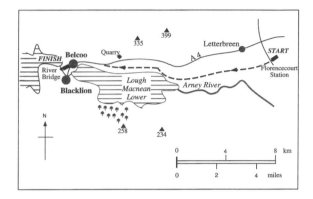

behind the lake and beyond them rises the long outline of Cuilcagh Mountain on the Fermanagh-Cavan border. This view is almost mirrored by a range of low, wooded hills on the right. Initially the road runs straight, through undulating country, crossing a number of tarred roads. At each intersection stands a large house, which must have evolved from more humble level-crossing gate-lodges of the railway days. Oak and beech trees were beginning to leaf on the warm, humid May day that I walked, and flowering hawthorn and crab-apples trees in the hedges combined to produce a strong, fragrant smell of early summer.

Halfway along the track rises, turns sharply through a reverse curve and quickly falls again in a cutting, a manoeuvre which certainly must have put the locomotive through its paces. As the eastern end of Lough Macnean is approached, the dairy fields become more reedy and cliffs in the hills overlooking the lake can be distinguished. The public road finally ends where the track runs beside a farmhouse as Lough Macnean is reached.

The trail carries on along the northern shoreline of the lake as a farm track. In parts it runs on the level between tall

hawthorn hedges, sometimes as an embankment (occasionally ploughed back into a field, but always recognisable).
If sections of it are wet or overgrown, the lake shoreline or
adjacent fields can be used to make more rapid progress.
Sleepers and original railway-crossing gates can be seen in
the hedgerows and a number of stone bridges carry the track
over streams that run into the lake. Gradually Lough Macnean
disappears from view as the track leaves it to join the main
road for the last kilometre to Belcoo. There is a large
quarrying operation on the hillside beside the road which is
the source of the constant low rumble that pervades the
region. Initially, the track runs beside the road, separated by
a low stone wall and then the path runs on a broad grassy
verge on the left-and side.

Although Belcoo village itself is unremarkable, it is
situated in an attractive location on a bridge of land between
Upper and Lower Lough Macnean. The presence of the
village right on the border is signalled by a huge, fortified
police base, dominating the hinterland. The village railway
station is on the road to Belleek and has recently been
restored and landscaped with the aid of a grant. It is in
impressive condition: a stone station-house, twin platforms,
spruced-up signal box and water tower base. Across the road
from the station the track continues through some fields for
half-a-kilometre down to the river that flows between the
two lakes. It was at the river crossing that the railway entered
the Republic of Ireland. The bridge that stood there was
blown up some years back for security reasons, but its upper
girderwork can still be seen, half sunken in the water.
Consequently Blacklion, on the other side of the border,
must be reached by the road-bridge. Both villages are small:
Belcoo has more shops, though Blacklion has more pubs (and
better ones at that!). The road-bridge which links the villages
is a restful location to contemplate the day's journey, with the

Belcoo station, County Fermanagh

evening mist rolling down from the Cavan mountains to the lake.

STAGE 2: Belcoo to Cornacloy

Distance: 12 km.
Time: 4.25 hours.
Start: Belcoo village.
Finish: Derelict level-crossing lodge at Cornacloy.
Description: A walk through the unfrequented landscape of north Leitrim.

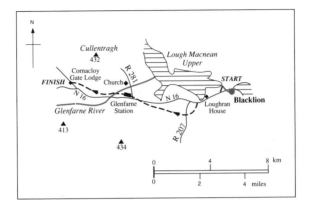

Leaving Belcoo, take the road bridge to Blacklion in County Cavan. Follow the road westwards out of Blacklion; the dismantled railway girder bridge over the river and the embankment that follows it will be on your right. For the first 2.5 km out of Blacklion a wide, new road has been built on the track bed. The original road, which has extensive housing on it, is parallel and to the left. The new road skirts alongside Lough Macnean Upper at a small lakeside park and jetty and the south Fermanagh hills can be seen on the opposite shoreline. Beyond Loughran House, an institute for young offenders, there is a road marked for Dowra. It is near this point that the track bed reappears faintly as an embankment in the fields on your left. There is a wide, but hidden, drainage channel between the road and the embankment, so the best policy is to walk down the Dowra Road for about 1 km and join the track at the level-crossing lodge. The lodge is a whitewashed, stone cottage with green gable boards and a distinctive porch at one end of the building. This style is reflected in all the gatekeepers' lodges on this section of line.

The track starts as an animal path through some marginal, agricultural land. There are some considerable curves and gradients on the way, with deep cuttings and tall embankments. The latter offer excellent views over Lough Macnean and the individual, rounded peaks of the mountains in north Cavan and Leitrim. A tarred road is crossed and the accompanying lodge has an incongruous mixture of the traditional and the modern, hens running in and out the open front door and a high-tech TV satellite dish perched on the chimney!

The track runs alongside the Sligo Road on an embankment and continues until you enter Leitrim and, by definition, the province of Connaught. Yet another gate-lodge is encountered, though this building has been abandoned to the elements. Shortly after, the first obstacle of the day appears, a missing bridge over a small river flowing into Lough Macnean. This interruption is particularly annoying as it occurs just as Glenfarne station comes into view. The nearby road can be taken to cross the river and the track rejoined immediately. From the embankment on the approach to the station a dancehall, "The Ballroom of Romance", can be seen, though I'm not sure that this is the one that inspired William Trevor's story of the same name! At the station there is a missing bridge over a road and the remaining sidewall stone abutments are a fine example of that particular construction.

Glenfarne station, 7 km from the start of the walk, is a surprisingly large complex with a limestone station-house, parcels office across the platform, and goods warehouse. It has been well-maintained, and the wooden verandas at the front and back of the station building survive intact. The only possible aesthetic quibble would be with a thoughtless kitchen extension protruding onto the track.

After Glenfarne station, the track leads to the Glenfarne River. Unfortunately, the bridge is no longer there and the river is most certainly not crossable at this point as it runs in a steep gully. Thus a short detour is necessary: take the road beside the station up and around a corner and past a Catholic church. The first laneway on the left after the church will lead down towards the track, which can be accessed through a field. This will enable you to join the track beyond the site of the former bridge.

For the last 5 km the track runs through more rolling country in a valley between two long, forested mountain ridges. It rejoins the Sligo road at the end of the small village of Glenfarne, 1 km west of the station. In the main, it makes its way on a ledge above this road, as a farm trail with beech and hawthorn hedgerows. Some of the cuttings are quite deep and may be wet, and one cutting in particular is heavily infested with gorse. The fields on the right or road on the left can provide alternative ways forward. A dismantled railway bridge, simultaneously passing over a farm road and stream, has to be negotiated but it presents no real problem. Scrapped motor vehicles have been dumped in some of the cuttings, a practice that is quite widespread in old railway lines through-out the country. This is somewhat ironic given the major part that cars played in the demise of the rail network!

The walk can be finished at another derelict gate-keeper's lodge on a road to Kiltyclogher, 150 m from the main road. This termination point is arbitrary and some ramblers may prefer to continue for a while on the remaining 8 km to Manorhamilton.

Lough Mourne to Barnesmore

and

Cloghan to Glenties

The County Donegal Railway (CDR) was the most extensive narrow gauge system in the country, and comprehensively covered the southern half of Donegal. The railway encompassed a number of separate lines with the twin towns of Stranorlar and Ballybofey being the hub of the system.

One of the first lines to be built ran south-west from Stranorlar, over the Barnesmore Gap in the Blue Stack mountains, to Donegal town. The line was opened in stages, most of it in 1882, though the last few miles to Donegal town were not completed until 1889. The route traversed some fine scenery through an isolated part of the county.

An extension westwards ran from Stranorlar along the River Finn valley to the small town of Glenties. This line was opened in 1895 and once again passed through some picturesque scenery in the so-called Donegal Highlands.

Typical of the remote lines in the west of Ireland, profitability was poor, especially with the advent of bus and car. The CDR is remembered as a progressive company and valiantly attempted a fightback with the pioneering replacement of steam operation by diesel railcars. However, by the middle of this century closure was inevitable. The Glenties branch closed first, to passengers in 1947 and to freight in 1952. The Donegal town line succumbed later, in 1960, along with the total closure of the whole remaining system. Sadly, the north-west of Ireland, from Sligo to Derry, is now completely denuded of all rail transport.

Three days' walking have been chosen from the network. The first walk is over the Barnesmore Gap, in the middle section of the Donegal town branch line. It starts near Lough Mourne, 6 km from Ballybofey, and finishes at the southern end of the Barnesmore Gap, 10 km from Donegal town. Donegal or Ballybofey/Stranorlar make equally good bases for this walk and there is a bus service between the two. Both towns can provide accommodation and food facilities, but, in my opinion, Donegal has the edge on Ballybofey/Stranorlar, thanks to its more agreeable location. The site of Donegal station is at the northern end of the town and it is now used as a bus depot. The stone station building has been restored as a Railway Heritage centre with photographs and film footage of the line in its heyday. Stranorlar station was sited beside the bridge over the River Finn and is also currently in use as a bus station. Unfortunately, there is hardly a trace of the original station buildings remaining and the fine railway bridge over the Finn has been lost as well.

Two consecutive stages have been picked from the western end of the Glenties branch. The first begins at Cloghan, a hamlet 12 km up the Finn valley from Ballybofey. It finishes at Fintown and the second stage continues from there to Glenties. Either Ballybofey/Stranorlar or Glenties can be used for overnight stays on this line. There are also limited possibilities at the two intermediate hamlets of Cloghan and Fintown. A short section of narrow gauge track has been re-laid at Fintown by the Central Gaeltacht Railway Society, and a restored diesel service was inaugurated in June 1995. The promoters had hoped to obtain the local celebrity, Daniel O Donnell, to perform the opening ceremony but had to be content with an official from their sponsoring board. The organisers have ambitious plans to eventually switch to a steam run and to extend the reopened railway all the way to Glenties! Donegal's railways may be gone but their heritage is being reawakened from a long sleep.

Part of the re-laid narrow gauge track at Fintown, County Donegal

Maps: OS (ROI), Sheet 11 (Discovery series); OS (ROI), Sheet 3
(half-inch series).

STAGE 1: Lough Mourne to Barnesmore

Distance: 11 km.
Time: 3 hours.
Start: Lough Mourne water treatment works.
Finish: Site of Barnesmore station at southern end of the
  Gap.
Description: A memorable walk through Barnesmore
  Gap in the Blue Stack Mountains.

The Lough Mourne water treatment works is on the left-hand
side of the road to Donegal town, 6 km from Ballybofey, on a

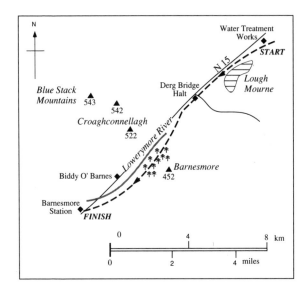

plateau of the Blue Stack Mountains. Looking to the north the narrow Finn valley can be seen, while ahead the two peaks of Barnesmore and Croaghconnellagh frame the Gap. Barnesmore is easily identified as it has a TV transmitter on its summit. The railway track is 30 m from the road and runs alongside a forestry plantation. It climbs up the mountain slope as a ledge, embankment and cutting and then the path levels out as it reaches Lough Mourne. For 2 km it runs along the lake shoreline on an embankment, and the beech grove planted during its construction is still healthily present. There are a multitude of stone culvert bridges over streams flowing into the lake and the larger Red Burn bridge is met towards the end of the lake. The opposite shoreline is bare moorland, though there is extensive forestry on the slopes of Barnesmore Mountain beyond. Leaving the lake, the terrain becomes more open as the track runs on a high bog plateau in a series of shallow cuttings and embankments. The planted beech trees give way to sporadic willow and gorse shrubs. Parts of the bog may be wet underfoot so care should be exercised. If the going gets tough you can take the road, as the main thoroughfare to Donegal town is a constant companion to your right.

The site of Derg Bridge halt is reached at a road over-bridge on the track. This is the highest point of the walk and there is a continuous fall in altitude as you proceed through Barnesmore Gap. There is no obvious sign of a platform here but, as compensation, there is a great view through the Gap of the distinctive outline of Benbulben Mountain in County Sligo. Rather more worrying is the evidence at Derg Bridge of the widespread problem of stone being illegally removed from the side walls of old railway bridges.

After this section, the track becomes indistinct for a little while and takes the form of an almost imperceptible cutting beside the main road. It is likely that the widening of this road has encroached on the track reservation. There is also potential confusion in deciphering the track's direction from markings in the bog from turfcutting. Luckily, the track soon clearly reappears as a forestry road on an embankment that curves away from the main road at the entrance to the Gap. The road carries on through the valley while the railway track runs on a ledge on the mountainside high above the valley floor. The northern side of Barnesmore Gap is empty and wild with the red granite rock on the bare mountain summits being quite conspicuous. This same rock was used for the track ballast underfoot.

The trail progresses through a thick, mixed spruce and larch plantation as a forest road and then returns to the open hillside in the centre of the Gap. It continues through the heart of the pass, overlooking the meandering Lowerymore River and the road in the valley below. As with most parts of this section, the path is very clear with hardly an obstacle to trouble the rambler.

The trail reaches the southern end of the pass, separated from the Lowerymore by a stone retaining wall. Beech trees reappear on the trackside and more gentle pasture replaces the wild heather. The famous Biddy O' Barnes pub can be seen down on the road, where the path goes through some deep rock cuttings and between a long grove of beech and hazel. A number of tributaries of the Lowerymore River are crossed, one of them tumbling down a magnificent waterfall beside the track. There are ridge and furrow marks on the track bed, the legacy of the timber sleepers.

A tarmac road leading down to the main road (and Biddy's!) is crossed. Those ramblers not tempted to stray from the path will find that after the grove the railway converges with the main road, eventually crossing the road. This was the original site of Barnesmore station, but not a trace has survived. The track continues on but gets a little more cluttered and most walkers will find that they are happy to finish here for the day. Having already spent one night in sleepy Ballybofey, I returned unexcitedly to it again.

STAGE 2: Cloghan to Fintown

Distance: 14.5 km.
Time: 4.5 hours.
Start: Bridge over the River Finn near Cloghan Upper.
Finish: Fintown station at Fintown.
Description: A walk up the River Finn valley through the Donegal Highlands.

Take the road to Glenties from Ballybofey (R252) and, a little less than a kilometre before Cloghan Upper, you will

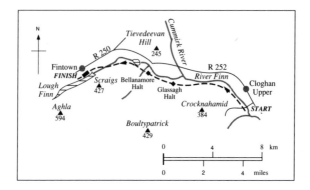

come to a small road on the left. This road crosses the River Finn at a bridge and on the other side of the bridge is the railway track where the walk commences. The track runs as cuttings and embankments through poor farm land on the south side of the Finn river. Hawthorn, willow and ash grow in the hedges and through them can be seen the northern foothills of the Blue Stack mountain range. Cloghan hamlet, perched on the hillside opposite, is passed and the track becomes a tarred farm access road which climbs westwards up the valley. At a T-junction, the track resumes its natural state and runs through open moor hillside with a forestry plantation ahead. The Finn is never more than 50 m away on the right and in parts the track proceeds on a ledge immediately above the river. The trail passes through a brief dark-green, spruce plantation as a grassy bank and then re-emerges on to the moor. Progress is rapid with intermittent barbed wire fencing being the only troublesome aspect. Scraigs and Aghla mountains, standing south of Lough Finn, loom on the horizon and a fine, stone road-ridge where the Cummirk River joins the River Finn can be seen to the right.

Presently the gently falling hills that form the river valley give way to a featureless bog plateau. Telegraph poles leaning at random angles illuminate the path ahead through the plain, and man-made markings in the bog demonstrate that turf cutting is being carried out. A concrete footbridge over the River Finn carries a small path from the main road down to the railway track. There are the barest of remains of a small stone platform along the track here and it is probably the site of either Elatagh or Glassagh halts. In the later years of old Irish railways, especially in the narrow gauge system, extra halts were added to the line in an attempt to more effectively compete with buses which could, of course, stop anywhere on their scheduled route. These halts were generally very modest affairs, sometimes no more than a name-board.

The river now begins to meander, freed from the corrective presence of the hills, and the track heads straight for (and through!) another short, fragrant spruce plantation, once again as a grassy bank. On the other side of this wood a bridge over a mountain tributary of the Finn is missing and boots must be removed and the river forded.

The track continues through the bog and comes to Bellanamore halt. This must have been a more glorified stopping place with a long single platform and corrugated iron shed surviving. Shortly after the halt, the track crosses a tarred road. Also at this point, the neighbouring Finn River splits in two, the left branch intersecting the track 150 m further along. Unfortunately, the bridge has been taken down and as the river is wide and deep here, it is not fordable. Therefore, take a detour to the left at the tarred road after Bellanamore halt, and, approximately 100 m along the road, turn right. This soon crosses the left branch of the Finn and the railway track can be rejoined easily via the bog. The trail runs on a low embankment along the south side of a small lake. Large, square timber posts stand in regular arrangements on the trackside, all that remain of farm-crossing gates. The track becomes a path on a curved ledge above the bog and passes a dilapidated redbrick gatekeeper's lodge at a tarmac lane. The trail rounds a corner formed by an outcrop of Scraigs Mountain. Its previous north-west course now becomes a south-west orientation which holds true all the way to Glenties.

Once around the corner, the northern faces of Scraigs and Aghla mountains open up on your left, their impressive steep cliffs tumbling down to Lough Finn. The main branch of the River Finn reappears on the right as the track heads for another spruce plantation. This is a striking section with the walker hemmed in by mountain cliffs on the left and the river to the right. Unfortunately the river must be forded on foot (thankfully for the last time on this walk!), as the bridge over it has been dismantled. The track proceeds as a gravel forest road through the coniferous plantation and comes out at the eastern end of Lough Finn, where it runs on a ledge alongside the lake through some small cuttings blasted through quartzite rock. A mature beech copse beside a graveyard is passed and the track then opens out into Fintown station. The stone station-house, water tower and goods-shed are standing and are in excellent condition, having been refurbished as part of the railway restoration project. Fintown is merely a hamlet, strung along the road to Glenties, but it has shops, pubs and a bed-and-breakfast. It is only a two-minute walk from the station.

STAGE 3: Fintown to Glenties

Distance: 14.5 km.
Time: 4 hours.
Start: Fintown station, beside the lake.
Finish: Glenties station, outside the town on the road to Letterkenny (R250).
Description: A walk through the moorland of west Donegal.

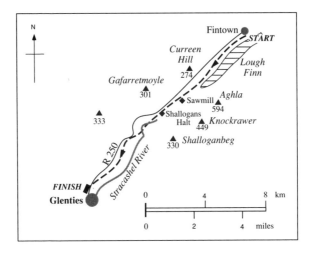

The initial section of this walk from Fintown station is along new track laid by the restoration society. It then becomes a gravel path leading to the western end of Lough Finn. This lakeside stretch of 4 km is a highlight of the walk, leading along the edge of the narrow lake with Scraigs and then Aghla mountains forming the stark backdrop on the other side. A number of stone bridges over lake-bound streams are crossed and the walker will be relieved to learn that on this walk all the bridges on the line survive intact! The road to Glenties (R250) is just to the right of the track and remains there for most of the walk. Near the end of the lake the track turns a gentle corner at a spur of Curreen Hill and, leaving the lake, becomes a grassy path under Aghla mountain.

For a section the trail becomes indistinct in the soft bog and the adjacent road may be more useful if the going is difficult. The track quickly reappears though, as a low embankment in rocky moorland surrounded by low brown hills. The long ridge of mountains continues to your left and the blue peaks of the Glencolumbkille peninsula manifest themselves on the horizon ahead. The track runs on the moor as a farm path or sheep-grazed embankments, invariably parallel to the road. A large sawmill is passed and, shortly after, a river that accompanies the railway for the remainder of the journey comes into view on the left. It flows westwards, down to Glenties, thus indicating that the Lough Finn watershed has been crossed. At a point where the mountain ridge on the left falls away, the site of Shallogans halt is met. This is slightly over halfway from Fintown and all that remains is the outline of a single, low platform. The Glenties Road then curves away in a lazy loop, while the track continues in a straight line as a forestry road through a young plantation. Free from the attentions of the road, it celebrates its independence by displaying the only major engineering feature on this part of the line: the crossing, and subsequent re-crossing, of the adjacent river by two large, single-arched, stone bridges.

You then pass through a cutting and a great view opens up down the widening valley to Glenties and over the mountainous Glencolumbkille peninsula. The path takes the form of a farm way and falls away sharply, while the Glenties road returns to your right. The track is now on the valley floor, passing through poor farmland and the occasional spruce plantation. It goes straight through a farmyard and under the only road overbridge on the line, a stone construction with brick facing. For a 500 m stretch, just after the bridge, the course of the track runs through bog and is indistinct; the neighbouring road may be needed. As it passes over a stream, conditions improve and it runs first as a gravel path and then as a grass bank through a long grove of hawthorn trees. You cross a tarmac road and the cottage there must have been, at one time, a gatekeeper's lodge. The track continues on through the grounds of a small factory and then it becomes a tarred road for a brief period as it meets the main road outside

Glenties. The station is only 200 m down this road, behind a hedge on the outskirts of the town. The whitewashed, stone goods-shed and distinctive station-house behind it are easily visible. Glenties, with one main street, proudly boasts about its early victories in the Tidy Towns competition on prominent display boards. Although its glory days are clearly over, it does offer opportunities for an overnight stay.

North Donegal

Barnes Gap to Burtonport

The Londonderry and Lough Swilly Railway (L&LSR) Company was responsible for the railway network in north Donegal, linking Letterkenny and the Inishowen peninsula with Derry city. The entire system was narrow gauge with the headquarters in Derry, which subsequently became part of Northern Ireland, though almost all the track lay in County Donegal. In 1903 an extension was completed connecting Burtonport, a busy fishing village on the Atlantic coast, with Letterkenny. The line, which took a roundabout route, was almost 80 km long and must have been the most remote railway in the country, running through wild and lonely terrain. Serving very small and separated communities, its construction required financial assistance from the government.

Leaving Letterkenny, the line initially ran westwards up the River Swilly valley before turning sharply northwards and heading through the Barnes Gap on its way to Creeslough village. Beyond Creeslough, it turned again and set an almost continuous south-westerly course for Burtonport, advancing across open moorland and having intermediate stations at Falcarragh, Gweedore and Crolly. The significant engineering feature on the line was the long Owencarrow viaduct lying between Barnes Gap and Creeslough. In 1925 high winds in this exposed region blew two carriages off the viaduct, killing four people.

Normal service on the line was two trains each way daily, with the journey between Letterkenny and Burtonport requiring something over three hours. Notwithstanding the very poor roads in the county, competition from trucks and buses gradually made the railway's position untenable. The western portion of the line between Gweedore and Burtonport was closed in 1940 while road fuel rationing during World War II helped delay closure of the remaining line to Letterkenny until 1947. Interestingly the L&LSR itself became involved in road transport and even today its buses, bearing the name "Lough Swilly", can be seen on the roads of north Donegal.

Over its western end, a distance of 54 km from Barnes Gap to Burtonport, the line runs almost unbroken through moorland. Therefore, given the near total absence of intensive farming and other types of development, the track bed permits a long and continuous walk. The only major interruption is around Creeslough where the line has become overgrown. Since the walk is mostly through bog it is best attempted during good weather after a long, dry spell; following prolonged rain a bog is almost impassable.

For convenience, the ramble has been divided into four consecutive stages though, naturally, any walker can arrange his or her own itinerary. The first day's walk is from Barnes Gap to Creeslough over the Owencarrow viaduct. The next three stages are: Creeslough to Cashelnagor station; Cashelnagor to Crolly; Crolly to Burtonport. Between Creeslough and Crolly the track runs along the northern face of the Derryveagh Mountains and there are good views out to sea. The last stage to Burtonport is through the flatter lakeland of the western coast. The start of the walk, at the entrance to Barnes Gap, is about 16 km north of Letterkenny, the largest town in Donegal. It has good bus links with Derry and Dublin, is well known in the north-west for its nightlife and has plenty of eating and accommodation options. The old L&LSR station building and goods sheds are still standing at the top of the main street and now contain the offices of the bus depot. The museum in Letterkenny has an exhibition on the Burtonport extension.

Maps: OS (ROI), Sheets 1 and 2 (Discovery series).

STAGE 1: Barnes Gap to Creeslough

Distance: 11 km.
Time: 4 hours.
Start: Site of Barnes halt on the N56 road.
Finish: Creeslough station.
Description: Some fine scenery and spectacular railway architecture.
Shorter Alternative: Barnes Gap to the Owencarrow viaduct (6 km).

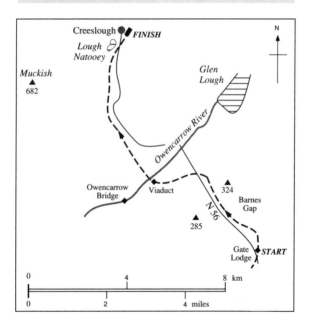

The walk is best started where the railway track crosses the N56 from Letterkenny, prior to entering Barnes Gap, at a point about 2 km north of Termon hamlet. The gate-house stands on the right-hand side of the road and the low embankment leading to it can be seen in the bog. The gatehouse also served as a stopping point for trains and was commonly known as Barnes halt. After the level-crossing the track runs as a farm lane, curving away from the road and gaining in height on embankments and cuttings. It then runs along the side of a low mountain ridge overlooking the plain below and makes a final climb in a long, curved cutting, blasted through igneous rock, at the entrance to Barnes Gap. For the next 2.5 km in Barnes Gap, the track and road run together, with the former sometimes alongside the road and in other parts running above the road on a ledge. The Gap is a long, thin valley in rocky moorland with bog cotton and wild orchids growing on the track bed. At the end of the pass the track originally crossed the road by a stone bridge which has since been taken down. The walker now needs to clamber down to the road and up the opposite side. The granite piers of the bridge, 15 m tall, are still present and indicate that the structure must have been an impressive sight in its day.

On the other side of the road the track continues through another very deep cutting and advances along a hillside on ledges and embankments. There are excellent views over the Owencarrow valley, Glen Lough to the east and the Derryveagh mountain range to the west. The distinctive rectangular outline of Muckish Mountain squats on the northern horizon. The trail is generally clear although there are patches of gorse on the embankments. A lane runs at the base of the track and can be taken to avoid difficult areas. A long, curved embankment, waist high in soft ferns, brings the track out into the river valley and on to the Owencarrow viaduct. The 300 m long viaduct carried the railway over the valley formed by the meandering Owencarrow River. While the viaduct has been dismantled, the many stone piers that supported it remain in position in the flat grassy bog on

The bridge at Barnes Gap, County Donegal

either side of the river. Making your way down from the embankment, you can walk through the grass to the river edge. There is a magnificent view west, straight down a long glen in the Derryveagh mountains. Unfortunately the river is too deep, well over 1 m, and its bed too soft to be forded. Instead you should head west along the river bank for 1 km to a road-bridge. When you reach the bridge, known as the Owencarrow Bridge, you can walk back along the river to regain the railway embankment on the north side of the Owencarrow.

For the final 4.5 km into Creeslough, the path runs close to and parallel with the main road. You can take the track bed for the first 3 km but the last part is best completed on the road. The railway runs through the flat bog below Muckish Mountain, crossing a number of small roads. Given the flat terrain there are few prominent cuttings and embankments and the track keeps a low profile. In the main, the way is clear and walkable, though some of the cuttings are overgrown with willow and hazel trees and the adjacent bog provides a faster avenue of progress. Gradually the trail becomes more infested and you may prefer to take the shortcut through the bog. There is a pleasant stretch as the track skirts to the east of Lough Natooey on an embankment and shortly after that it crosses to the eastern side of the road at a level-crossing. Creeslough station is to the right of the junction where the main road bends sharply left just before entering the village. The station-house, beside the golf course, is a long, single-storey structure and, as with most railway buildings on this line, is pleasant if not particularly distinguished. Creeslough village is a small and serviceable overnight base.

STAGE 2: Creeslough to Cashelnagor

Distance: 14.5 km.
Time: 4.5 hours.
Start: A point on the track, 2 km north of Creeslough.
Finish: Cashelnagor station.
Description: A memorable day's walk through the empty moor at the foot of the Derryveagh mountain range.
Shorter Alternative: Creeslough to Falcarragh station (9 km).

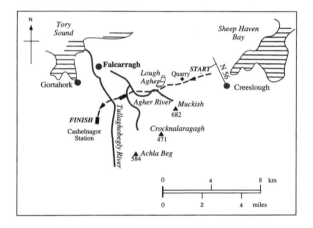

This stage begins just outside Creeslough because the track is either overgrown or built on within the immediate vicinity of the village. Take the N56 north and then the first road to the left at a junction 2 km out from the village. Follow this small road until you come upon the railway track on your left, about 250 m from the road. The track has just performed a ninety degree turn from its previous orientation and now heads almost due west towards Falcarragh station.

It runs along a hill as a farm lane, offering command-ing views over the region. The sea inlet at Creeslough, known as Sheep Haven Bay, can be seen to the east and beyond it the faint outline of the mountains on the Inishowen Peninsula. On the southern horizon is the ridge through which the previous walk in the Barnes Gap pro-gresses, while ahead is the sharp summit of Muckish. The path continues through shallow cuttings and embank-ments, drawing close to the road and eventually running alongside it. Then you pass two gate-houses at level-crossings. Most gate-houses, assuming they have not been extended or renovated beyond recognition, are identifiable by their relatively tall and narrow shape. Parts of the way are over-grown with furze and the adjacent bog or road may need to be used. After passing a large quarry, the track veers away from the road. From here until Falcarragh station, the track bed is completely clear, making it an easy stretch of railway walking.

The path runs below the north face of Muckish mountain through desolate moorland, devoid of any signs of human culti-vation or habitation. The track construction consists of rocky cuttings, precarious ledges and magnificent embankments – tall, long, curved and cambered – which drag the line along the side of the mountain. All the while the track bed is on a continuous, gradual ascent. You regularly encounter round pillars, built from loose stone, at the side of the track. These were probably posts from sheep-crossing gates which have long since been removed.

Progress is unhindered and rapid and you are soon on a ledge which runs along the southern shoreline of lonely Lough Agher. Black basalt can be seen in the cuttings, and the streams at the edges of the track are a reddish-brown, which indicates iron in the rock. Beyond Lough Agher the line descends progressively as it leaves the scree-covered western slopes of Muckish. The Agher River and its many tributaries, which flow westwards from the lake to the Atlantic, are crossed on stone and girder bridges. Civilisation unassumingly reappears in the shape of houses on the distant hills. Tory Island with its distinguishing, craggy outline can be spotted out to sea and the village of Falcarragh on the coast. With Muckish Mountain behind you, the other peaks in the Derryveagh range come into view.

A small level-crossing lodge is encountered next and then the track starts to run on a gravel road. Shortly before Falcarragh station it crosses another mountain stream. Luckily for the rambler, almost every bridge on this unique line is still present and, apart from the Owencarrow, the tiresome business of fording streams is not necessary. In addition, the latter half of the section from Creeslough to Falcarragh is completely without fencing on the track, which makes it exceptionally walker-friendly. Falcarragh station is 3 km south of the village which must have proved rather inconvenient for its inhabitants. Of course this inconvenience also extends to present-day ramblers who wish to finish their trek here! Like the station in Creeslough, it is a long, single-storey building with the platform intact.

After Falcarragh station the going becomes slightly more difficult as the track runs through more low-lying and wetter ground. The railway turns south-west and for the 5 km to Cashelnagor station proceeds along the north face of the Aghla Beg and Aghla More mountains, notable for their striking profiles. The way runs through moor and poor agricultural land, in parts as farm lanes and in others as rough bog roads. Sections of it are wet and/or overgrown and the neighbouring moor must be taken, which can make your progress quite slow. The Tullaghobegly River is crossed and the track gradually gains in altitude. It turns due south in a long cutting in the bog, heading directly for Errigal

Mountain, then along a wide, flat valley between Tievealedid Mountain and Errigal.

Presently Cashelnagor station can be spotted straight ahead, all alone in the moor, and the track reaches it via a shallow cutting. The station-house is gaunt and derelict, in the middle of a wild, exposed bog surrounded by mountains. It is certainly the most isolated station that I have come across; the nearest settlement is Gortahork, 4 km to the north on the road from the station. Perhaps when the railway was built this area was more populated, but in any case the remoteness engenders a sense of eerie charm. On a more prosaic matter, terminating the walk at Cashelnagor will pose a problem for those ramblers without transport. However, given the course of the line, this dilemma is unfortunately unavoidable.

STAGE 3: Cashelnagor to Crolly

Distance: 14.5 km.
Time: 5 hours.
Start: Cashelnagor station.
Finish: Crolly station on the N56.
Description: A long walk over the moor and then through wide valleys in the hills.
Shorter Alternative: Cashelnagor to Gweedore (10 km).

The track leaves Cashelnagor as a tarmac road, then becomes a farm lane beside a house. It runs through very marginal farmland and passes two small lakes on either side of the track, the surfaces of which are almost hidden by water lilies. There are also many ruins of stone cottages in the area which indicate that at one time the region was not so deserted. Tory Island can be seen again, and this time the lighthouse at its western extremity is quite evident. The line reaches a summit along this section before a long descent to Lough Nacung.

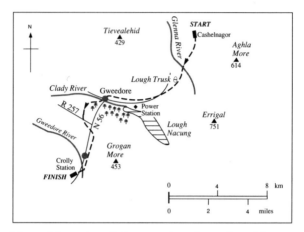

Many of the rock-walled cuttings have been adopted for use as sheep pens by placing gates at both ends. The track reaches and passes under a small road; the bridge here is unusual in that most road and railway intersections on this particular line are level-crossings.

Beyond the road the trail descends through a rough river valley at the western foot of Errigal. The terrain here is more rugged than the flat bog prior to Cashelnagor and the track weaves between two squat, steep and rocky hills. For the first 200 m the line proceeds indistinctly between two stone walls but then runs along a fine embankment, with a stone bridge over the Glenna River. The railway cuts into a hill as a thin ledge and subsequently becomes a long shallow cutting. It then runs along the edge of Lough Trusk. All the while you are overshadowed by the impressive Errigal, to all the world resembling a Hibernian Matterhorn. The land flattens out as the track starts to head for the main N56 road. The path is on open bog where the marks of the sleepers in the soil are still visible. Where the line crosses a sheep track stands a gate-lodge, which seems a somewhat extravagant gesture on the part of the railway company. I did not complain, however, as it provided a very fortunate and satisfactory shelter from a sudden heavy cloudburst. Normally in open moorland such cover from the elements is non-existent.

The path carries on, descending steadily, and soon becomes a turfcutters' track before intersecting the main road. Lough Nacung, situated in a long valley, comes into view with the forested slopes of Grogan More behind it. After crossing the main road the track continues through the bog on the hill, parallel with and above the road, as both head for Gweedore. There is a super view from the hill eastwards up the Glenveigh valley. The track bed then passes Gweedore power station on the lakeshore. In parts, the way is gorsed over or wet and the road is a useful alternative. Many sections are clear though and the track runs on grassy, rather than heathery, moorland. Towards Gweedore, at the western end of Lough Nacung, the lake narrows and the track becomes cluttered with buildings. Consequently the final half-a-kilometre to Gweedore should be undertaken on the road. Both coniferous and deciduous trees are present on the hills giving the area a more welcoming feel than the barren country walked previously. Gweedore is simply a T-junction in the road and its prominence on the map is surprising as there is no village there at all. The site of the station is behind a house on the right-hand side of the road. Very little remains, except the twin platforms which indicate that there was a passing loop here.

At Gweedore the track turns south over the Clady River; the bridge has been dismantled, though its piers remain standing in the river bed. Take the road until it crosses the river and for just over 1 km thereafter, then take the second lane to the right. You pass a water channel for Clady hydro-electric power station – the construction of which, a decade or so after the railway closed, has obliterated the track bed completely for a stretch. The track can be found again at the end of the lane just before another bridge over the channel. The trail progresses as a clear gravel path through the bog, affording good views over the bay and the islands within it and, more incongruously, over the large and needlessly conspicuous industrial estate at Gweedore. As a striking contrast to the line before Gweedore, the countryside and roads here are liberally dotted with uniform white bungalows. This part of the west coast of Donegal is densely populated by rural standards and is the largest Irish-speaking region, or *gaeltacht*, in the country. The path crosses the Bunbeg to Crolly road (R257) and makes straight for Grogan More Mountain. It changes into a grassy track and then intersects the N56 again where there is a well-maintained and stylish gate-lodge.

From here the railway runs close to the road, on the hillside, into Crolly. However, it has been pervaded with dense tree growth and gorse so the walker should remain on the road for the short distance into the village. Crolly is a haphazard ribbon-like settlement on the main road and, like other centres in this region, seems to have been allowed to develop without the benefit of town planning! Take the road to the left, just before the bridge over the Gweedore River, where the railway track can be found at a level-crossing, approximately 300 m along the lane. The track progresses along a rocky cutting, then over a stream and a tall bridge over the Gweedore River. It meets the N56 again at which point we come upon Crolly station, a two-storey, inhabited building with an accompanying platform. It is slightly less than 1 km south of the village of Crolly which has a large pub and a summer restaurant, plus bed-and-breakfast accommodation.

STAGE 4: Crolly to Burtonport

Distance: 14 km.
Time: 4.25 hours.
Start: Crolly station.
Finish: Burtonport station beside the quay-side.
Description: Flatter terrain than the previous two stages, with the walk ending on the Atlantic coast.
Shorter Alternative: Crolly to Kincasslagh Road station (10 km).

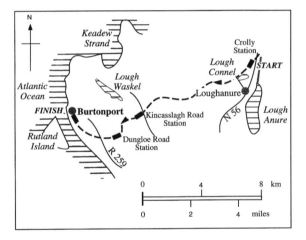

From Crolly station, walk along the road for 30 m and pick up the track in the bog. At first its reservation is unclear, but it soon takes on a more defined shape as an embankment along the road. The course of the line is through hilly country, overlooking the Gweedore River as it enters Lough Anure. Presently the track curves away from the road through two low hills and makes in a westerly direction for Burtonport.

It proceeds as a narrow foot track through a short valley and comes out over Lough Connel, then runs on a red granite ledge along the northern shoreline. Small sections of the line are overgrown with furze bushes but it is worth persevering through these difficult passages as the way is generally free. Towards the end of the lake the going does get tough, so come out onto a convenient minor road. There is a gate-house where the railway crosses the small road to Loughanure village. I had my, by now customary, chat with its occupier who kindly looked after my bicycle for me.

For the next 3.5 km a small public road, with a grass "nature-strip" running down its centre, has been laid on the track bed. The mountains are finally left behind and for the remainder of the journey to Burtonport the track goes through rocky moorland dotted with innumerable small lakes. On this road section only the presence of the occasional rock cutting reminds one that this route was once a railway line. The road eventually comes to an end at a railway under-bridge and the track compensates for the easy road walk by entering a long and impassable cutting. Luckily another road, which runs alongside the railway, comes to the rescue. After some housing the track improves and can be rejoined at a level-crossing lodge, with magnificent, large gateposts standing defiantly in the bog.

The walk continues on a grass path through the moor, passing over a granite road underbridge. In parts the line may be wet or populated with willow or furze and sections may need to be skirted. Views begin to appear of Keadew strand on the coast and hilly Aran Island, which lies offshore from Burtonport, can be seen ahead. The sighting of the latter, with steep cliffs on its northern perimeter, indicates that this long journey is drawing to a close. Crossing a road we arrive at Kincasslagh Road station with its granite station building, platform and neighbouring gate-lodge – all in pristine condition. The history of the line, and of this particular station, was retold to me by its current owner. Apparently after the Burtonport extension was built the citizens of the village of Kincasslagh, belatedly recognising the advantages accruing from the railway, demanded that a station be built at a point on the line closest to them. Hence the subsequent construction of Kincasslagh Road station in 1913.

It is 4 km from Kincasslagh Road station to Burtonport. The track climbs and falls through the bog and skirts scenic Lough Waskel. Many small roads are crossed though without any signs of gate-lodges. The hills on the Crohy Head Peninsula can be seen to the south and, far beyond them, the mountains on the Glencolumbkille Peninsula can be distinguished jutting out into the Atlantic. Again parts of the track are clear while other, thankfully shorter, portions have returned to nature and must be avoided. The approach to Dungloe Road station is an example of the latter and, to compound the frustration, the station itself is mundane and not greatly worth the effort. The track then curves northwards, crosses the main Burtonport to Dungloe road (R259) and begins to run alongside the seashore. For the last kilometre into Burtonport another road has been built on the track bed. This is a lovely section and, luckily for the rambler's tired legs, is an undemanding end to the walk. The road runs over a number of small causeways at the edge of Rutland Sound, with rocky Rutland Island across the short sea channel. Beyond it lies the more prominent island of Aran with the extensive housing on its eastern seaboard clearly visible. The road meanders through fish-processing buildings as it enters Burtonport Harbour and then the derelict station looms on the right-hand side of the road.

Burtonport is essentially a large fishing harbour but it has pubs, restaurants and some limited bed-and-breakfast accomodation. Through a quirk of history it is not Irish speaking, though it is sited at the western extremity of the Donegal *gaeltacht*. While ferries leave from the quay-side for Aran Island, most tired railway walkers will be considering heading back east rather than continuing further west.

Clogher Valley

Tynan to Maguiresbridge

The Clogher Valley Railway (CVR) was a narrow gauge line that ran for 60 km through rural Ulster, mostly in south Tyrone. The eastern terminus of the line was at Tynan station on the main Great Northern Railway (GNR) Clones to Belfast line, while the western terminus was at Maguiresbridge on the GNR Clones to Londonderry line. It was opened in 1887 and was the first line to be built under the Tramways Act, which promoted railways in the more remote regions of Ireland. For the most part it ran along the existing roadside, either on a raised grass embankment or behind a hedge. The exceptions were generally where the road gradients were too steep and the railway required its own reservation. There were seven intermediate stations on the line; Aughnacloy, Ballygawley, Augher, Clogher, Fivemiletown, Colebrook and Brookeborough, plus numerous smaller halts. In the early years of this century, there were four trains daily each way and the journey time was two-and-a-half hours. The partition of Ireland in 1921 led to some complications for the railway, for though it lay entirely within Northern Ireland, the line in effect ran along the border, especially at its eastern end. With the onset of road competition in the 1920s the railway's fortunes declined rapidly, though it limped on until its final official closure in 1941.

The defining characteristic of this walk is that it is predominantly a roadside walk and thus avoids most of the rigours of cross-country walking. A good part is actually on minor roads, as subsequent road developments mean that, for some sections, the railway no longer runs alongside the main road. Although the track bed has been removed from the route, the chain of station-houses and level-crossing gate-lodges provides the necessary ingredient of nostalgia. One of the attractions of the walk is the insight it gives into the unique and intensely local aspect of life along the frontier between North and South. The many pleasant villages on the way are another appealing feature of the walk, and most have preserved their distinctive historical character. Many of the villages were originally laid out as hill plantation towns in the seventeenth century. They prospered until the middle of the nineteenth century, when the inexorable growth of Belfast meant decline for the smaller cottage industries.

The entire walk takes three days. The first stage is north-west from Tynan station to Ballygawley along the Tyrone and Monaghan border. The second day is a long journey from Ballygawley to Fivemiletown at the western end of the Clogher valley. The final section takes you from Fivemiletown to Maguiresbridge near the shore of Upper Lough Erne. Most of the villages on the route can provide accommodation and have public transport links, while the starting point at Caledon can be reached by local buses from Armagh which, in turn, has regular connections to Belfast and Dublin.

Maps: OS (NI), Sheets 18 and 19 (Discoverer series); OS (ROI), Sheet 8, (half-inch series).

STAGE 1: Tynan to Ballygawley

Distance: 21 km.
Time: 5.5 hours.
Start: Tynan station, 1.5 km from Caledon on the Middletown Road (B210).
Finish: Ballygawley station, at the roundabout in Ballygawley.
Description: A walk along the Blackwater river-basin, parallel with the border.
Shorter Alternative: Tynan to Aughnacloy (14 km).

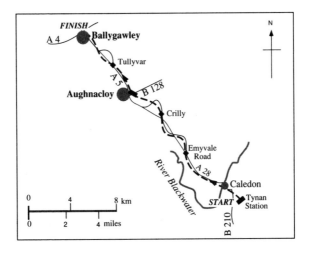

The GNR station-house at Tynan, although now derelict, is still an impressive gothic building. It can be approached by a driveway up from the Middletown road. The signal-box, wooden footbridge, goods and locomotive sheds, and the main line platforms are still standing. The curved platform edge of the Clogher Valley line can be made out, just to the right of the station house, flush with the surrounding ground. The whole complex now serves as an untidy farmyard.

At the foot of the driveway on the Middletown Road is an interesting, three-storey corn-mill dating from 1844. Turn right at this point and follow the road until it meets the Armagh to Caledon road (A28). The Lemnagore level-crossing gate-lodge stands at this junction; it is a redbrick cottage with a slate roof, porch and decorative brickwork over the doors and windows. A track leads back from the lodge towards Tynan station, an embankment that carried the line over the small Tynan River by means of a single-arched stone bridge. Some railway sleepers are still visible on the bridge.

Follow the road over the Blackwater River, which marks the county boundary, and then up the hill into Caledon. The entrance to the Caledon Estate is passed on the left and beside it stands a plinth which is all that remains of an obelisk blown up by the IRA. There was no station in Caledon and the railway ran along the main street and stopped across from the now empty court-house. Caledon has some fine, period buildings and some terraced architecture reminiscent of Bath.

From Caledon to Aughnacloy, a distance of 13 km, the railway mostly ran along a raised verge on the left-hand side of the road. However, only the first 5 km of the walk, to the site of Emyvale Road halt, is on the main road because after that the railway ran along what have now become minor roads. The initial stretch from Caledon is on a curvy, sycamore-lined road with a wide grassy verge. The combination of rolling, open meadows, mature, deciduous trees and large, imposing farm buildings exude an air of agricultural prosperity. Along stretches of the road, parallel rows of ash and elder ditches mark the path of the railway bed on shallow embankments or cuttings. The meandering River Blackwater, which forms the border with County Monaghan, is at some places less than a kilometre to the left. From Emyvale Road halt, currently occupied by a machine shop, a small road winds down to the river and, although the main bridge was blown-up by security forces, a footbridge gives easy access to the Republic. It is a jolting reminder of how much the Troubles has impinged on the life of the border communities.

For the next 5 km, to Crilly hamlet, the track follows a quiet country lane, initially curving to the right and then crossing to the left of the main road (A28). Crilly, where the railway made another stop, is just to the right of the main road. The road then rises steeply past a disused quarry. A derelict stone gate-lodge on the right, with similar features to the lodge at Lemnagore, marks the spot where the railway track leaves the road on the final stretch to Aughnacloy. A pine grove embankment carries the track over some low-lying marshy ground, and railway-crossing gates can be seen in the side ditches. A series of deep cuttings and embankments drag the railway up a steep incline until it runs close to the Aughnacloy to Benburb road. At the outskirts of Aughnacloy, cross over to this road which will bring you into the station at Sidney Street.

Aughnacloy station is a two-storey, redbrick building and was the headquarters of the Clogher line. The station-house itself is now used as a municipal playschool and the platform in front of it is in excellent condition. The extensive station yards and sheds were used until very recently as an army base. Aughnacloy, as befits a busy market town, has a respectable number of pubs, shops and restaurants and so makes for a good lunch spot. As with all the villages I passed through, the line is remembered by the old and imagined by the young with great affection. I was inundated with plenty of humorous anecdotes about the operation of the railway and its alleged foibles! As you leave Aughnacloy, look to the west for superb views of the Monaghan hills.

The railway rejoins the road just outside the town and for most of the remaining 6.5 km to Ballygawley the track runs on the verge to the right of the main road (A5). There is a steady, continuous climb to Tullyvar halt, halfway between Aughnacloy and Ballygawley, which is now a maintenance depot. At the fork in the road take the minor road to the left where you will see the track continue, just over the hedge. Halfway up the hill there is another gate-lodge on the right-hand side of the road. It is empty, but not boarded up, and the interior is still in good condition. The original gate-lodges had two rooms on the ground floor and a narrow stairway which led up to two bedrooms. They must have been warm and snug residences although by today's standards they appear quite small.

At this point the railway deviated cross country, although it is easier to continue on the minor road which leads to a small cross-roads and then rejoins the main road at Tullywinney gate-lodge. The railway also came back to the road at this point before descending into Ballygawley along the right-hand verge. Major road construction has removed most of the infrastructure at Ballygawley station, situated just to the west of the large roundabout. However, a single-storey building on your right survives, with a distinctive round window in its side gable. Ballygawley was disappointingly smaller and quieter than I had expected and certainly no gourmet paradise! The only food option was a take-away, but there are six pubs from which to chose. Of these, Gormleys, a very old-fashioned bar run by a town stalwart, is really the only one of note. Its sloping formica-topped counter is reminiscent of 1950s coffee bars and it is quite unusual these days in not having any draught beer; drinkers must be satisfied with bottles.

STAGE 2: Ballygawley to Fivemiletown

Distance: 22.5 km.

Time: 6.5 hours.

Start: Ballygawley station at Ballygawley roundabout.

Finish: Fivemiletown station at the western end of Fivemiletown main street.

Description: A walk through the heart of the Clogher Valley.

Shorter Alternative: Augher to Fivemiletown (15.5 km).

The unappealing, and very busy, main road west to Enniskillen (A4) must first be taken for 2.5 km. The raised embankment of the railway, now planted with two rows of trees, can then be reached by crossing the reedy field to the right. You

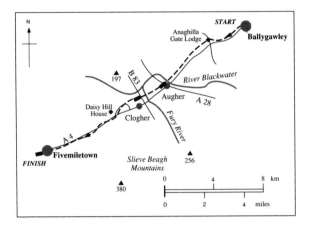

encounter a small stream which must be crossed before the embankment becomes a cutting, currently used as a farm track. The sides of the cutting are peppered with thistles and snowdrops and it brings the trail through the side of a hill. Cross a small road at what was Annaghilla gate-lodge and continue on the track bed over a small railway culvert bridge where sleepers and, more unusually, some old narrow gauge rails can be seen in the ground. Finally, a modern chicken farm blocks the way and the main road must be rejoined. The railway line lies just over the hedge on the right-hand side of the road and after a while it is possible to rejoin the track for the remaining 3 km to Augher. A GAA pitch stands close by and the track is neatly utilised as a grassy spectator embankment.

The Blackwater River is crossed again prior to entering Augher and marvellous scenes of the lazy river meandering through woodland can be seen from the bridge. A pub, prominently advertising itself as "The Railway Bar", occupies one of the corners at the crossroads at Augher and diagonally across from it is the single-storey, redbrick station-house. It is currently a restaurant and is a good spot to stop for a coffee and leaf through the railway memorabilia that the staff have kept.

Clogher is a further 3 km from Augher and involves a walk along a paved footpath on a grass reservation beside the road. This was the original path of the railway and has thus, rather inadvertently, become one of the very few old tracks in Ireland to have been converted to a pedestrian walkway. Leaving Augher the spire of Clogher Cathedral pricks the western skyline, while to your right Augher Lake and Spur Royal Castle can be seen. Walk into Clogher, crossing the Fury River, and take the first road to the right (B83) to Clogher station, now a sawmill, which stands across from the cattle mart. It is a two-storey, redbrick building with twin gable ends that face towards the platform. Clogher has an ancient ecclesiastical heritage and boasts the smallest cathedral in Ireland. The main street is on a steep hill and hence the railway skirted it to the north. It is halfway to Fivemiletown and thus a sensible place to take a lunch break. I got chatting to the owner of a pub, who had on display an old Clogher Valley Railway ticket and an original Sale of Lands deed to the Railway Company dating from its construction. A working lunch so to speak!

Recommence the journey at Clogher station. Remain on the road and walk past the cattle mart where a spruce embankment indicates the path of the railway. The large, stone building which can be seen in the distance to the north-west was a paupers' workhouse. Once you get closer to it you can see the ultimate destination of its unfortunate inmates – a graveyard with a scattering of yew trees to your right. Across from the graveyard is a house and behind it the track continues as a muddy sheep path. Two minor roads are crossed, with the path metamorphosing into a curved grassy cutting and then into a gravelled road. Many of the distinctive level-crossing gates that once guarded the line where it crossed public roads are encountered on this section. Clogher army base, with its frequent incoming and outgoing helicopter border patrols, is on the hill to the left. The minor road, reached through a farmyard, was the old Enniskillen road; the railway ran along the verge on the left. A small country stream is crossed and you can see the gate-lodge to Daisy Hill House. Eventually, you reach the main road where a signpost informs you that you have 8 km to go to Fivemiletown!

Proceed along the main road for half-a-mile, then take the small turning to the right. This is yet another short section of the old road and it winds past some derelict farm buildings and two small lakes lined with ash trees, which are home to the swans and coots that bob placidly on the water. This relaxed interlude is all too short and soon you are back on the A4. For the remainder of the journey the railway ran on the verge to the left of the road. At Fivemiletown, it famously ran down the middle of the narrow, busy main street, and must have created quite a commotion! The town library contains an exhibition on the railway line. The station building, which is a twin to that in Clogher, is now part of a creamery and in very good condition.

Fivemiletown, one of the largest villages in the Clogher Valley, has plenty of accommodation, restaurants, shops and pubs, and the front room of the "Select Bar" on the main street is a particularly cosy example. My companion and I reminisced on our long day's walk in front of an open fire whilst listening to the cheery gossip of the bartender.

STAGE 3: Fivemiletown to Maguiresbridge

Distance: 16 km.
Time: 5 hours.
Start: Fivemiletown station.
Finish: Maguiresbridge station, outside the village on the road to Florencecourt.
Description: A short, pleasant walk in east Fermanagh.

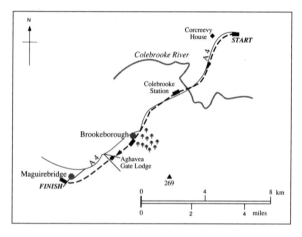

It had been snowing heavily as we entered Fivemiletown the previous evening and continued to do so through the night, so we commenced this final stage with a pervasive white carpet covering the ground. The snow combined with the dotted spruce plantations and the hills on the northern and southern skylines combined to produce an unexpected low Alpine vista. The village of Brookeborough lies 10 km to the south-west and, unfortunately, the first half of the walk to the village is on the gravel hard shoulder of the main road.

Leaving Fivemiletown, the large ruin of Corcreevy House is seen on the right. Shortly after that the road enters County Fermanagh and crosses the watershed from the Blackwater to the Colebrooke river basins. About 3 km further on the main road can be dispensed with and the small road to the right should be taken. This road, which was the original Enniskillen road, crosses the Colebrook River by an old stone bridge and then passes an entrance to Colebrooke Estate, home of the late Sir Basil Brooke, a long-serving prime minister of Northern Ireland and equally long-serving chairman of the Committee of Management of the Clogher Valley line! The railway track can be seen 50 m away on the left, running through a coniferous wood and leading to Colebrooke station. This was the smallest station on the line and, although not purpose-built for the estate, had all the attributes of a private station.

Shortly after the station, the road rejoins the A4 but, rather than follow the main road, walk straight across it and take a pleasant hillside detour through Brookeborough. (Purists, of course, will prefer to stay on the main road as that was the path of the original line.) Slieve Rushen, on the Fermanagh and Cavan border can be seen ahead and to the right is the valley through which the railway ran. Brookeborough, with an attractive backdrop of forested hills, is quickly reached. At the war memorial in the main street, bear right down to the main road where, just around the corner and over a hedge, a somewhat overgrown embankment can be distinguished. You can clamber onto it without any great difficulty and follow it as becomes a long grass cutting, gracefully curving into Brookeborough station. Brookeborough has the best preserved platform of all the Clogher Valley stations, though the actual red-and-puce-brick station-house is now uninhabited and for sale. The tidy village itself doesn't have much in the line of food possibilities though the nicely-fronted "Brokenspoke" pub will offer some respite.

The final 6.5 km stretch to the western terminus now lies ahead. Take the old road to Maguiresbridge for half-a-mile. It leads to two identical cottages, 150 m apart. The trains were unable to cope with the gradient ahead, and so now had to take their own route through the countryside. This has become a farm track that leads through some fields and then across a newly-cut drainage channel (which must be jumped over!). The track crosses a minor road at Aghavea where Aghavea Glebe Cottage now stands, presumably converted from the original level-crossing lodge. The track bed runs on a shallow embankment, bringing the line over swampy, low-lying ground, and then meets another road-crossing. Beyond this second road, the railway course becomes pretty impenetrable and it is wise to take the road to the right which brings you up to the main Enniskillen road leading to Maguiresbridge.

When you arrive walk up the main street and bear left at the road signposted for Florencecourt. Maguiresbridge GNR station is only five minutes along this road on the right-hand side though, regrettably, it is in much poorer condition than its sister terminus at Tynan. Most of the once-extensive goods-sheds have been flattened in the derelict site, though the brick station-house is still standing. The two mainline platforms, being more resistant to such "redevelopment", are still in good order. Once your curiosity has been satisfied, retrace your steps to Maguiresbridge to partake of its hospitality. There are also good bus links to nearby Enniskillen.

North Antrim

Martinstown to Retreat

and

Ballycastle to Capecastle

The first narrow gauge railway lines in Ireland were built in County Antrim, before government assistance became available for such projects. The oldest line was the Ballymena Cushendall and Red Bay Railway (BC&RBR) which, in adopting a three-foot gauge, fixed the width as the future standard for the national light-railway network. The line, completed in 1876, left the main line at Ballymena and climbed up over the high ridge of the Antrim mountains to finish at Retreat.

The railway was originally built to exploit iron ore deposits in the mountains and provide a means of transporting them to the coast at Cushendall. The line belied its name, however, as it never reached the sea: the gradients proved to be too severe. In getting as far as it did, the railway attained a summit level which exceeded 305 m, making this the highest track in the country. Initially the line carried only freight but a passenger service was subsequently inaugurated as far as Parkmore station. In 1903, the railway passed into the hands of the Northern Counties Committee (NCC), which was owned by the Midland of Britain. Passenger services eventually stopped in 1930, though freight transportation survived for a further decade.

A neighbouring, narrow gauge line with a similar history was the Ballycastle Railway which opened in 1880. It left the main line at Ballymoney, the next major station north of Ballymena, and ran from there in a north-easterly direction to Ballycastle on the north coast. Shortage of funding meant that the line was built cheaply and profitability was always pre-carious. The railway was almost closed in 1924, which would have made it the first narrow gauge closure in the country. Luckily, it obtained a reprieve and survived until 1950 when it succumbed in the era of mass closures.

One walk has been chosen from each of these lines. On the Cushendall line I have selected the stage from Martinstown, up through the glen, to Retreat which lies on the other side of the mountain. The village of Cushendall, although just beyond the end of the walk, is without doubt the most scenic base from which to approach this excursion. There are good bus links to Belfast, Larne and Ballymena, plenty of places to stay and eat, and some excellent old-style pubs. A shorter walk is taken from the second line, starting at the railway terminus in Ballycastle and finishing at Capecastle. This walk is along the western slopes of Knocklayd Mountain and Ballycastle is an obvious, and worthwhile, choice for a base – having all that a rambler could demand. Two alternative bases could be the large towns of Ballymena and Ballymoney respectively. Both are still on the rail network but rather lacking in character, though the station building and accompanying pub in Ballymoney have a charm that has been rewarded with prizes in railway competitions.

Maps: OS (NI), Sheets 5 and 9 (Discoverer series); OS (ROI), Sheet 2 (half-inch series).

STAGE 1: Martinstown to Retreat

Distance: 12 km.
Time: 4.25 hours.
Start: Martinstown, a hamlet on the A43 from Ballymena.
Finish: Site of Retreat station on the B14.
Description: A long, mountain railway walk.
Shorter Alternative: Cargan to Retreat (8 km).

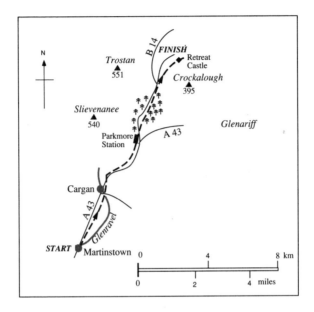

At the small hamlet of Martinstown, a dismantled rail-bridge over the Glenravel Water can be seen beside the Glensway Tavern. Walking up through Martinstown, the track can be joined at the northern edge of the village, running to the right of the road (A43). The track makes its way up the valley, running along a ledge that has been cut into the hill above the Glenravel River. A large church and some adjoining houses have been built on the track and must be skirted around using the road. The trail then runs on a low embankment through some reed-speckled fields. The track becomes a gravel road for a short section as it passes some polythene greenhouses, behind a belt of spruce trees. A number of small drainage channels have been cut into the track; they should pose no problem, although I carelessly fell into one!

As the line approaches Cargan, the valley acquires a more pronounced form, with low mountains on the forward and side horizons. The track skirts a GAA park, then passes through a grove of cypress trees beside the car park and playing fields. Leaving the sports park, it takes the form of a solid embankment which curves around a meadow. Curiously the land improves here, with fine mixed woodland more characteristic of rich lowlands. The track again crosses the Glenravel River on a magnificent high embankment and then follows a series of cuttings through hayfields. It ends at an impassible road overbridge on the outskirts of Cargan, and you should take the road into the village.

The track runs behind the houses to the right of the road in a deep, overgrown cutting, before crossing the road at a Maxol garage. As at Martinstown, there seems to be no identifiable station building in Cargan, perhaps because those in authority thought a freight line required little in the way of station infrastructure. There is a restaurant and pub and a brief rest at this point is recommended because the remainder of the walk is through wild and exposed moorland.

The trail can be picked up again just outside Cargan, on the left of the road. It climbs steeply up the glen on embankments, ledges and cuttings between the road and the Cargan Water. Some of the cuttings are through bog while others must have required blasting through rock. The track is well defined and the going is clear and easy through the grassy moor. Other tracks can be distinguished on the mountain side, perhaps the remains of those short, but extensive, industrial lines built to serve the small iron ore mines in the area. There are a number of derelict houses along the way, indicating that the area was formerly more densely populated. Although the line lacks any grand railway architecture, there are some fine stone bridges over the track and a few smaller ones over mountain streams. Near the summit, at Parkmore station, forest plantations appear on the slopes to break the barren terrain.

Parkmore station, the terminus for passenger traffic on the line, was the highest, and probably the most isolated, station in the country. The station area is rundown, though the station building survives with its prominent name-board intact. The water tower is also in a very good condition and not only has the brickwork survived well but, more surprisingly, the metal tank remains in place. Just after Parkmore the adjacent road forks; the A43 veers off down the mountain to Glenariff, while the B14 and the railway trail continue over the plateau to Cushendall. The main climb has been completed, but the railway continues to ascend gradually over the next 3 km, prior to its precipitative fall on the other side of the mountain. It is probably easier to take the road for about 800 m from Parkmore station until you come to a rail underbridge where the track can be rejoined.

The line runs on a very high, clear embankment through a dense coniferous wood and the ground underneath is soft with a deep coating of pines, needles and twigs. At a dismantled bridge is an impressive, granite abutment which is over 7 m tall. The many ferns which grow over and around the buttressing almost hide its facade, giving it the appearance of a lost Aztec temple in a jungle. The embankment gradually gives way to a long cutting as the track rejoins the roadside, and there is a fine, single-arched, brick bridge which carries the railway over a stream. The track proceeds along the road with forestry on either side, sometimes as a gravel track or as a damp cutting. (One disadvantage of rambling near forestry in summer is that the walker is plagued by swarms of persistent flies and midges.) Eventually, the railway reaches the end of the forest with the upper slopes of Trostan Mountain, the highest peak in the Antrim range, on your left. This marks the point where the track reaches its maximum altitude and begins the descent down the open glen towards Retreat.

The path is momentarily indistinct due to the bog but soon manifests itself as an unmistakable cutting, close to where the neighbouring road forks again. The track falls sharply in a long, continuous cutting and then runs along an embankment. A breathtaking view opens up over the glen, and the Mull of Kintyre can be seen across the sea channel.

A lone and dilapidated building on the hill marks the site of Retreat station. On maps this area is marked as Retreat Castle which is certainly much too grandiose a title for the building that currently stands there. I assume the castle has been pulled down, but no further information on this subject was forthcoming when I asked some local people. After the station the track continues for about 500 m through a shallow cutting before petering out on a hill, but it is worth walking this distance for the superb view over the glen and Cushendall. Retrace your steps back to the station and take the farm lane out to the public road leading to Cushendall, 5 km away.

STAGE 2: Ballycastle to Capecastle

Distance: 5 km.
Time: 1.5 hours.
Start: Fair Hill Road in Ballycastle.
Finish: Capecastle station site near the A44.
Description: A short walk through agricultural land in north Antrim.

The site of Ballycastle station, behind the town's main street, now serves as an Ulsterbus depot though, unfortunately, none of the original buildings appear to have survived. The walk starts at the top of Fair Hill Road and leads past the cattle mart. From the top of the road you can walk back 100 m to the four-arched, sandstone rail bridge over the Tow River, but the track is completely sealed off on the other side of this

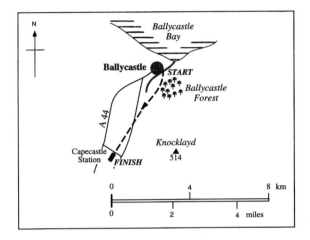

bridge and you need to retrace your steps in order to begin the walk proper. Take the gravel path which is part of the Moyle Way trail along Ballycastle forest. The trail runs under a road overbridge and it carries on through a cutting and along a hill ledge overlooking a small river in the valley below. Shortly after this, the Moyle Way curves away to the left, leaving the walker with a more arduous task.

The railway track continues on an embankment, initially grassy but all too quickly becoming smothered with gorse. The next kilometre is quite difficult and it is best to take a farm lane that runs at the base of the embankment through the fields. The embankment advances through mixed woodland on the lower slopes of Knocklayd mountain and becomes progressively less cluttered. A number of brick bridges over cattle trails are encountered; some are intact but others have not fared as well. Luckily, the latter are not insurmountable. From tall sections of the embankment the rambler can look back on the town and out to the Atlantic ocean to catch glimpses of Rathlin island. A minor road from Ballycastle to

177

Capecastle is traversed. The original rail overbridge no longer stands but a fine, side abutment survives.

Beyond this crossing the track clears up and there are some fine stretches on high embankments and deep cuttings. The trail proceeds through fertile, but very steep and rugged hill country on the western flanks of Knocklayd Mountain. It continues in a wide, curved reservation beside a brook and then on a shallow embankment in the fields. Even by disused railway standards, there are an enormous quantity of rabbits on this track. Although the gorse has disappeared, the regular presence of barbed-wire fencing across the track is an equally tiresome, though less problematic, impediment. Many farm-crossing gates with their sturdy concrete posts can be seen in the hedges and an unusual polythene sheep pen must be skirted.

As the track approaches Capecastle station it takes a deep cutting which is largely overgrown and it is better to take the side fields for this stretch. Just before Capecastle station the track enters a tunnel, 70 m long, straight and unobstructed, though wet underfoot. The tunnel takes the line under a road and the station is on the other side, in another cutting. Many stations on the light railway network were no more than halts and this must have been the case with Capecastle as there appears to be no signs of any railway buildings here. However, the platform has remained and the platform-edge stones can be clearly seen in the grass. From Capecastle, the track continues on through flat, low fields to Armoy and this is a pleasant, if unexciting, walk.

Newcastle to Drumadonnell

This walk is along a stretch of the Newcastle to Banbridge line in an extremely scenic area of Northern Ireland. Newcastle's station was built in 1869 as part of the Belfast and County Down Railway (B&CDR) network. Banbridge acquired a station in 1859, served by a spur from the main Dublin to Belfast line operated by the Great Northern Railway (GNR). By 1880 this spur line had reached Katesbridge and Ballyroney, just 16 km north-west of Newcastle. A period of rivalry then ensued between the two rail companies as GNR coveted some of the lucrative holiday trade from Belfast to Newcastle, which the B&CDR jealously guarded. A compromise was eventually reached whereby GNR extended its line from Ballyroney to Castlewellan and the B&CDR constructed a branch from its Newcastle terminus to Castlewellan. The line was built in 1906 making it one of the last substantial new railway undertakings in the country. Train services from Newcastle to Banbridge were run by the GNR with four connections each way on weekdays. There were five intermediate stations between Newcastle and Ballyroney: Castlewellan, Savages Bridge, Leitrim, Ballyward and Drumadonnell. As with all lines in Northern Ireland, it suffered from the severe anti-rail policy of the post-war Stormont Government and was closed in 1955.

Along with the Glens of Antrim, the coastal area of south Down is generally regarded as being one of the most beautiful regions of Northern Ireland. Its principal town, Newcastle, is set between the Mourne Mountains and the Irish sea, and still serves as a popular seaside resort for the inhabitants of Belfast. It is well equipped with food outlets, accommodation and public transport, but suffers from the associated drawback of being very busy at the height of the summer season.

The walk consists of two stages: the first is from Newcastle to the smaller town of Castlewellan, while the second continues on from Castlewellan, finishing at Drumadonnell station, half-way between Newcastle and Banbridge.

Maps: OS (NI), Sheet 29 (Discoverer series); OS (ROI), Sheet 9 (half-inch series).

STAGE 1: Newcastle to Castlewellan

Distance: 7 km.
Time: 2.5 hours.
Start: Newcastle station at the top of the main street.
Finish: Castlewellan station on Station Road.
Description: Primarily a walk on roads, along the
　　northern borders of the Mourne Mountains.

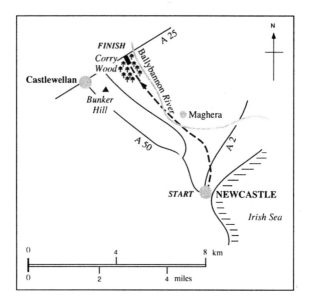

Even allowing for the stations that were built on mountainous peninsulas along the west coast of Ireland, the site of
Newcastle station must be among the most breathtaking
on the island. Passengers stepping out from the redbrick
terminus building would have seen a skyline dominated by
Slieve Donard falling sharply to the sea. The station building,
distinguished by a clock tower and green-topped roof, is
centrally located at the head of the main street and is now a
supermarket. Unfortunately, the line between Newcastle
station and Maghera has been almost completely removed by
urban development and agriculture. It originally ran alongside
the main Belfast road before crossing some low-lying ground to
reach a road-bridge to the west of Maghera. To reach this bridge,
you should now take the main road to Castlewellan (A50) and
then bear left at a hotel just outside the town. The road-bridge
at Maghera is a twin-tunnel, stone bridge and affords great
views of the Mourne Mountains to the west with wooded
Bunker Hill commanding the northern skyline.

From this bridge the railway followed a north-westerly
course to Castlewellan station. The track along this section
is partly in the form of an embankment but it is so overgrown
with gorse, furze and bramble that it is best to take the
parrallel minor road. Walk towards Bunker Hill, to where the
railway bridge over the Ballybannon River can be seen. As
the road progresses up the eastern flanks of Bunker Hill,
approaching Corry Wood, the vista opens up behind you.
This walk along a quiet country road is very pleasing, though
it certainly would have been even better if the planners had
had the foresight to preserve the old line as a pedestrian trail.

Presently you come to Station Road in Castlewellan. The
old station is a few hundred metres away on the right. The
derelict building lies just beyond the mature spruce plantation of Corry Wood but is surrounded on all sides by a
scrap-yard. Stone buttressing on the steep clay sides of Station

Road marks the point where the railway crossed over the road. The hilltop town of Castlewellan is just under 1 km away with a selection of shops, pubs and restaurants.

STAGE 2 : Castlewellan to Drumadonnell

Distance: 11 km.
Time: 4 hours.
Start: Castlewellan Station on the A25.
Finish: The site of Drumadonnell station, 1.5 km east of Ballyward on the A50.
Description: A cross-country stage in south Down with no major obstacles.

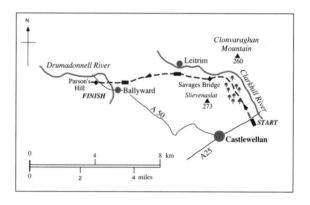

The walk can be commenced on the main Castlewellan to Downpatrick road (A25) to the east of Castlewellan. Stone buttressing on the northern side of the road signifies the site of a dismantled rail overbridge. Take the Clarkhill Road where you can access the track through some open ground between two houses on the left. Walk back towards the A25 and look across the main road at forlorn Castlewellan station, incongruously encircled by scrapped, Dublin city buses. Turn around and retrace your steps along the track until it peters out in a deep, waterlogged cutting. The Clarkhill Road should then be rejoined beside a small roadside shop and you can continue northwards along the road towards Clarkhill Wood. Before the wood, you come across a partly sunken, two-storey house on the right. Behind the house, the shallow embankment of the railway line can be seen entering the forest. This is the end of the road stage of the walk.

In the forest the trail starts off on an embankment and then in a cutting. Wooded stages of railway trekking always seem to produce a distinct sense of exaggerated solitude. The way becomes a dirt path with a carpet of leaves and twigs, running along the edge of the wood. After a few hundred metres, which coincide with a rusted level-crossing gate, it becomes a more elaborate, gravel track. Willow and ash trees act as sentinels on the path, while on the left is the large, coniferous Castlewellan Forest. Holly was very evident when I walked the route in February though it becomes more difficult to spot as the deciduous spring foliage returns. On your right the pastures cascade down to the Clarkhill River, while beyond the river rises a rugged hill, Clonvaraghan Mount. Its lower slopes are colonised by a spruce plantation but the rocky summit is covered in red-brown heather. An untidy, corrugated-iron fence signals the end of the forest and the track leads through a grass cutting to a single-tunnel road-bridge, now used as a rudimentary animal shelter.

Beyond the bridge a collection of farm outbuildings have been built on the track and they must be skirted via a nearby riverbank. This was the site of Savages Bridge station, but sadly no trace remains. For the next 2.5 km the track bed proceeds on level ground through a low valley just south of the Clarkhill River into the village of Leitrim. The track has been completely removed but by maintaining a straight line towards the spire of Leitrim's Catholic church, the walker will not go astray. The fields are inhabited by sheep, their presence challenged by the occasional group of bullocks. Sleepers and rusted railway wire may still be seen in the fences, and the old railway culverts can be used to cross drainage channels. Halfway to Leitrim the railway reappears in the form of a shallow embankment, its cropped grassy covering indicating extensive sheep grazing. Level-crossing gates, timber stiles, sleepers and ballast proliferate on this section.

The path becomes a farm track and then a deep rocky cutting as you approach the redbrick road-bridge at Leitrim. The bridge has characteristic brickwork on its sidewalls and offers excellent views of the Mourne Mountains. Leitrim village is only 300 m further along the road and merits the small detour. The village consists of a crossroads, a shop, an old stone warehouse and two pubs, one of which was being painted in a garish sky blue as I passed. Leitrim station can be found just beyond the bridge but it is a rather sorry structure, having suffered the ignominy of being converted into a cattle pen. However the station-house and platform are still there.

Rough grass covers the track and a stream can be crossed by a planked culvert bridge beyond the station. A farm track on an embankment brings you to the next road-bridge and further on is a series of deep cuttings through hill country. As the cuttings hold water in winter, it is easier to walk in the fields alongside them, though this necessitates the repeated crossing of barbed-wire fencing. Farmhouses dot the neighbouring hills.

Going under another bridge, you will follow an embankment over some low-lying, wet ground. A narrow stream presents a minor obstacle and the embankment continues to Ballyward station. The station is beside a small road and is in remarkably good condition. Both the signal-cabin and the inhabited station-house are built from timber and in good repair. The two, long platforms have also been treated kindly by time.

Remaining on the left-hand side of the track, it is best to walk alongside the deep, undergrowth-infested cutting rather than through it. Ballyward village, Anglican church and the main Castlewellan to Banbridge road (A50) are passed on the left. The trail becomes a muddy farm track on a tall embankment, with a bridge over the Drumadonnell river. The land here improves as the Mournes are left behind and the trail enters the river basin of the Upper Bann. A wide, reedy cutting leads under a road-bridge and shortly after that the Banbridge Road at Parsons Hill is reached. The original bridge is now gone but there are still good views of the Down hills at Dromara to be had from the road. On the other side of the road is the site of Drumadonnell station but, as with Savages Bridge, it has completely disappeared. Ballyward village is about 1.5 km back along the A50. There is a small shop here and a limited bus service to either Banbridge or Newcastle.

Cooley Peninsula
Fathom Forest to Greenore

I n 1873, a railway was constructed from Dundalk to the port of Greenore at the end of the Cooley peninsula. The intention behind the railway was to develop the port for boat services to England. Later the line was extended from Greenore, through Carlingford and up into Newry in 1876. At Dundalk and Newry, it made connections with the Great Northern Railway. The line was operated by the Dundalk, Newry and Greenore Railway Company (DN&GR) though it was actually owned by a separate English company throughout its existence. The railway never fulfilled expectations primarily because Greenore could not divert customers from the established ports. Cargo and cattle shipments were the main business of the line and the unprofitable passenger services were terminated very early – in 1926. Nor was the railway helped by the partition of Ireland in 1921. The company found that its operation was split by the new border, necessitating the introduction of cumbersome customs points. In spite of a take-over by the Great Northern Railway in 1933, losses continued and the railway was eventually closed in 1951.

The Cooley Peninsula lies between the north and south of Ireland, though most of it is in the Republic. It is an attractive, little-known corner of the country with Carlingford Lough on its northern shores, Dundalk Bay on its southern flank and the Cooley Mountains running down its spine. Cooley has its place in Irish mythology as the site of the famous Cuchulainn and Queen Maeve legend.

The walk can be reached via Newry which has excellent bus and rail links to both Belfast and Dublin. I have selected just one stage from the line, beginning at Fathom Forest, crossing the border and going on through Omeath and Carlingford to end at Greenore. It is possibly the most scenic section of the railway, providing great backdrops for a day's walk.

Maps: OS (NI), Sheet 29 (Discoverer series); OS (ROI), Sheet 9 (half-inch series).

Distance: 17 km.
Time: 5.5 hours.
Start: The car park and picnic site at Victoria Lock, 6.5 km from Newry, on the road to Carlingford (B79).
Finish: Greenore Village.
Description: A walk along the southern shores of Carlingford Lough. Mostly cross-country, though some sections are on the beach and there is a certain amount of road walking.
Shorter Alternative: Fathom Forest to Carlingford (13 km).

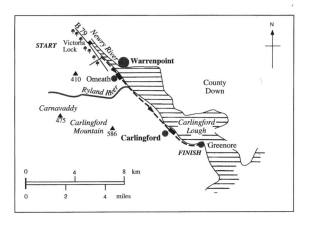

Victoria Lock is at the end of the Newry Canal, on the tidal Newry River. The main road to Carlingford now runs on the path of the railway track but the original, smaller road to

Carlingford is present on a ledge just above the main road. It runs along the edge of Fathom forest, where larch trees are much in evidence, and allows good views across the Newry River to County Down. Presently a derelict pub, Patsy's Parlour, is passed and the small road becomes a hard shoulder running alongside the busy main road. Straight ahead you can see the craggy outline of Carlingford Mountain dominating the northern side of the Cooley Peninsula. Perceptive ramblers will note that the road surface improves at a bridge over a small stream where the international boundary between Northern Ireland and the Republic has been crossed! The overgrown railway track is visible on the left of the road, passing over a small bridge and running right along the river estuary bank on buttressing walls. About 2 km from Victoria Lock you come to a crossroads and a large pub called Davey's. Turn left and, 20 m down the road, there is a bridge over a railway cutting at which point the track proper can be accessed.

The cutting is wooded with beech, ash, sycamore and the omnipresent whitethorn. Continuing on, the track becomes an embankment though while I was walking a bulldozer was levelling it with a neighbouring field. It is a pointed reminder of how fragile the walking resource of old railway lines can be – even fifty years after their closure they are still being broken up. The two round towers on the river bank are disused navigation lighthouses and, across the water, the extensive docks at Warrenpoint port can be seen. From here to Omeath station, the condition of the track bed is variable: some sections are walkable, but others are impassable and the sand and pebble shoreline must be used as an alternative. Shortly before Omeath, the railway runs through a wooded demesne where the timber sleepers and shale ballast are still present on the line. The track carries on through a public park and then Omeath station is reached. Located beside a sea pier, it consists of a single-storey, whitewashed station-house, in good order, and a short, low platform. From the pier, the Victorian frontage of Warrenpoint town can be seen across the Lough. Omeath village itself, 5 km from the starting point of the walk, is a haphazard collection of shops, pubs and houses strung along the main road.

Take the tarred road running along the sea front. The next 8 km to the town of Carlingford is a very scenic railway route, comparable to the best in Ireland. The track is sandwiched between the shoreline and the steep northern flanks of Carlingford Mountain. Leaving Omeath, it runs on a seadefence embankment, separated from the main road by a stone wall. The walker will encounter many groups, each of four stone pillars in a square, the remains of numerous cattlecrossing gates along the line.

The path passes through an empty and shabby caravan park before coming to the Ryland River. The bridge has been removed but the side abutments survive, and still look remarkably fresh. The river is shallow and easily fordable by foot, or there is a road-bridge 50 m upstream. Beyond the bridge the track is heavily overgrown and it is better to walk on the rocky shoreline of the lough. The hills are bare, with only a covering of heather, whereas across the water in County Down they appear more extensively forested. A "holiday village", dating from the 1960s, has been built on the track and must be skirted. Soon after, a small fishing quay is met.

From here to Carlingford the track is quite open. Some rock-blasted cuttings were obviously required for its construction, together with a number of bridges over the streams that flow into the lough. Rambling as I was in late April, there was an abundance of primroses, buttercups and bluebells on the track bed and I spotted a number of foxes, peering out warily from a copse of hazel trees. An unusual feature of the line is the black railing present along its edge for considerable sections. Presumably it was erected by the railway company, though it seems a rather extravagant gesture when compared to the more prosaic, but functional, hedgerows.

The trail becomes a laneway, leading into a marina and boatyard, 1 km outside Carlingford. On the approach into the town, a new wide road has been built on the path of the line. It runs through a wide cutting, under a large, brick-lined road-bridge, with King John's castle standing guard above. Carlingford station is further along, to the right of the main road. It is a twin-gable, stone building and was the largest intermediate station on the line. The exterior has been restored by the local authorities and a wall plaque outlines a brief history of the railway. The structure is now more mundanely employed to house both a public toilets and a health centre, which seem rather odd bed-fellows to have in the same building!

Carlingford is a suitable place to stop for lunch. The town has had an interesting medieval history and contains excellent examples of Norman urban architecture. Remaining somewhat unknown, the area still has a natural charm that is now missing from many of the heavily promoted west coast regions. On a more practical issue, accommodation should be arranged here because the destination of the walk, Greenore, has no overnight facilities.

Leaving Carlingford, the main road continues on the path of the railway over the next 2.5 km, through the flat eastern end of the Cooley Peninsula. You pass a grey stone level-crossing lodge on your left, its gable barge boards unmistakably proclaiming its identity. After a long straight section of road, deliverance is at hand and a curved embankment takes shape on the left. This carries the track into Greenore, passing alongside a golf course, and there are good views of the higher eastern peaks of the Mountains of Mourne. The embankment, running right along the sea, eventually stops at a dockside fuel depot (the rest of the track has been blocked off) and you can reach the main street of the village by walking past the clubhouse.

The railway station that stood on the quay at Greenore has long since been removed, but the large redbrick railway hotel can still be seen and, although it is in a rather sorry state, it retains an air of long departed grandeur. The main street of the village is mainly industrial stone terracing, lightened by the use of red and yellow brickwork, with an imposing shop and pub interspersed between the houses. The pub has a weathered mock-up of a DN&GR locomotive in its grounds.